A ZERO WASTE FAMILY

IN THIRTY DAYS

ANITA VANDYKE

APOLLO
PUBLISHE

A Zero Waste Family: In Thirty Days
First printed in the United States of America in 2022.

Apollo Publishers books may be purchased for educational, business, or sales promotional use.
Special editions may be made available upon request. For details, contact Apollo Publishers at
info@apollopublishers.com.

Visit our website at www.apollopublishers.com.

Published in compliance with California's Proposition 65.

Library of Congress Control Number: 2021949837

Text copyright © 2020 by Anita Vandyke.
Cover illustration and design, internal design, typesetting and illustrations by
Louisa Maggio © Penguin Random House Australia Pty Ltd.
Illustrations pp. 24, 63, 65, 74, 79, 85, 101, 106, 127, 152, 159, 165, 171, and 203 by Melissa Stefanovski.
Author photograph © Joi Ong.
First published by Penguin Random House Australia.

Print ISBN: 978-1-954641-12-9
Ebook ISBN: 978-1-954641-13-6

The wood used to produce this book is from Forest Stewardship Council (FSC) certified forests,
recycled material, or controlled wood. Controlled wood cannot be:

- Illegally harvested.
- Harvested in violation of traditional and civil rights.
- Harvested in forests where high conservation values are threatened.
- Harvested in forests being converted to plantations or non-forest use.
- Harvested in forests where genetically modified trees are planted.

CONTENTS

A ZERO WASTE FAMILY

IN THIRTY DAYS

Also by Anita Vandyke

A Zero Waste Life: In Thirty Days

To my daughter, Vivian,
who taught me not to waste my life.

INTRODUCTION

THE (PLASTIC) STRAW THAT BROKE THE CAMEL'S BACK

In the first year of my daughter's life, I was also reborn. Before Vivian's birth, I was the stereotypical type A personality with a five-year plan, a regimented morning routine and a daily schedule that was so tightly packed my assistant had to schedule in toilet breaks. Yes, this really happened: in my former life as a high-flying corporate engineer, my personal assistant had to schedule in five-minute breaks between back-to-back meetings to give me time to go to the toilet, eat, drink and do all the other essential things a human being requires. But all this fell to pieces when my daughter was born. Babies don't have a schedule, and they certainly don't give a rat's ass about your morning routine. Five-year plans? Pft, you can't even make a five-minute plan. This, you can imagine, was a shock to the system for a person like me.

On the outside, I was pretending I was still managing. I thought if I planned it all thoroughly and asked for help when I needed it, then everything would be fine. I was wrong. The pressure I placed on myself to have "it all" and look good while doing so, had turned my life into a pressure cooker waiting to explode.

This led to the "straw that broke the camel's back" incident. I was sitting down at my favorite café after a ten-hour day of work in a hospital. After almost a decade as an engineering manager, I had returned to study to earn a degree in medicine and was in the middle of a surgical rotation as a trainee doctor. I hadn't eaten all day and all I wanted was a green smoothie. Being "the zero waste girl," I said to the waiter, "No straw please, I am trying to reduce my waste" He nodded and smiled. "Of course, we need more people like you." I was an eco-warrior, the bestselling author, the happy mother, the diligent medical student. If you looked at the perfectly tiled pictures on my Instagram page, you'd think I really did have it all.

Then the smoothie arrived . . . and in it was a plastic straw. I immediately burst into tears. It was the literal straw that broke the camel's back.

I was inconsolable. You'd have thought *that* straw meant the demise of all sea life, that *that* straw was the cause of all the methane in our atmosphere, but really, what that straw represented was overwhelm. I was completely and utterly overwhelmed—by being a full-time medical student, by being a new mother, and by trying to live a perfect, zero waste life.

My tears represented the oppressive feeling in my chest that I wasn't doing enough, that I wasn't the best medical student, that I wasn't the best mom, that I wasn't being the most eco-conscious citizen. I felt like a fraud.

This sense of overwhelm is why I decided to write this book. As parents we are constantly juggling the needs of others, children, work, chores, and money. The state of the planet is the last thing on our minds. To make matters worse, plastic pollution, climate change, ecosystem collapse and the extinction of the bees (the bees!) is splashed across the media as if it is an inevitable apocalypse. What can we mere humans do if we are doomed to fail anyway? The writing of the book also overlapped with our lives being impacted by the events of 2020, when emotions were raw and society was trying to grapple with the social and environmental changes the year had wrought. It illustrated even more clearly to me that we are all juggling different priorities, and sustainable living has to be simple and seamless.

This is a book about how I learned to be a truly zero waste parent. I wrote my first book, *A Zero Waste Life: In Thirty Days*, about how individual changes can make a big cumulative difference when it comes to reducing waste. This book is focused on actions you can take as a family. By "family" I simply mean a group of people that you love. That can be a biological family, or one that you have created with the people you care about the most.

My definition of a zero waste life is about more than just a diet that does not produce plastic waste. It is about not wasting your life. To me, being a zero waste parent means not wasting time trying to be the "perfect" parent. Instead, zero waste living allows you to focus on the things that matter most: family, community and the environment. This book is a thirty-day guide highlighting the lessons I've learned during my first year of navigating motherhood while studying medicine and still trying to reduce my waste. It is a guide to how families can reduce their waste and also avoid wasting our lives worrying about things that don't truly matter. I want to show you that, by applying zero waste and minimalist principles to your life, being an eco-parent doesn't have to be difficult. In fact, it can be easy!

As I write this, my hair is unwashed, dinner isn't ready, the baby is crying and I haven't prepared for the exam I have tomorrow. I am tired.

This tiredness is more than just a general fatigue, it is a bone-tiredness that comes from sleepless nights and the guilt of not doing *enough*. Not enough for your child, not enough at work, not enough for the environment.

Enough.

Enough of that. This book is not designed to add to the guilt that we already feel as parents. It is about recognizing that everything you do is *enough*. Instead of just writing about reducing your waste, I want to give real solutions aimed at making your life easier. That's why the book is broken into three sections, organized according to the concept of the "ripple effect."

At the center is *self-care*, which then expands into *home care* and, finally, to *child care*. Self-care is placed at the core of the book, because if we don't put on our own oxygen masks first, how can we be expected to look after others? The first five days focus on putting in place habits that make *you* the top priority. This is done to improve your life, so you can improve the lives of those in your care.

As any parent can attest, we often place ourselves at the end of a very long list of people we need to take care of, and in doing so we neglect our own needs. Oprah has said, "I consider it a compliment when people say I am full of myself, because only when you're full—I'm full, I'm overflowing, my cup runneth over—can you have so much to offer and so much to give." That's the importance of self-care: to make sure your own cup is full, so that we can be more mindful and have more energy to attend to others.

After caring for ourselves, the next ten days are focused on home care and setting up habits designed to minimize your waste. This means minimizing waste in all areas, including resources such as time, money and energy, as well as cutting down on plastic and single-use waste.

The final fifteen days are dedicated to child care. I've created easy and fun life hacks for you and your children so you can all reduce your household waste while also having fun as a family. These hacks are designed to simplify your life and make the boring stuff (like chores) take less time, so that you can spend more time doing the things you love.

Since becoming a parent, I've experienced "parental guilt" on a regular basis. Unsurprisingly, this guilt has also expanded into other areas of my life, including a newly formed eco-guilt. For the first time ever, eco-anxiety has entered the psychiatric lexicon to describe the anxiety that we feel about the future of the planet. Eco-anxiety is a real thing, and it is not unfounded. We *should* be anxious about climate change, plastic pollution, dying ecosystems and mass extinction, but, rather than overwhelm us, this anxiety should fuel our fire to want to make a change, no matter how small. We don't need another thing to add to the guilt of parenthood, but we do need to appreciate that every small act leads to a bigger change—a change in mindset, a change in lifestyle and, eventually, a change in the well-being of our planet.

Reducing plastic pollution and lowering our waste is something we can all achieve in our everyday lives. These consistent actions can empower us to have more control over issues that often feel so out of our control. This book is a reminder that the easiest way to tackle overwhelming issues is to start with ourselves. The ripple effect is subtle, yet profound. By changing your day-to-day habits, you will start to feel that you are setting a positive example for your children. We are leading by example and showing that every person, no matter how small, can make a big impact on the world around them.

Throughout this thirty-day period, I want you to sprinkle some "Mama Magic" in your life. This is the special kind of magic that only parents possess. It involves adding a touch of creativity, enthusiasm and love to all your projects, including how you treat yourself, take care of your home and look after others. It's a practical magic that will make your home life fun again.

I've combined my knowledge from blogging on my Instagram account (@rocket_science), gathered advice from the zero waste community and used my own creative problem-solving skills honed through years of engineering experience to make this book for you. This is more than just a manifesto on how to reduce your waste as a family; it is a guidebook on how to make more time for the important things. Let's begin!

MY DEFINITION OF "ZERO" WASTE AND MINIMALIST LIVING

I explained in my first book, *A Zero Waste Life,* that the "zero" in zero waste living is just a goal and is not to be taken literally. To me, living a zero waste life is more than having just a plastic-free household. It means not wasting your life.

"Minimalism" often brings to mind a monk-like existence. However, I want to show you a new way of thinking about living minimally. I use minimalism to mean not consuming more than you need. Your family's needs might be different than those of my family. There is no judgment on what is defined as a "need." Rather, minimalism is a tool designed to make us reflect on the things that matter the most in our lives (and very often, they aren't *things*) and give you the freedom to live a simpler life.

This double meaning of a "zero waste life" is at the heart of this book. It means not wasting *any* of your resources, including plastic, money and, most importantly, time. Don't be daunted by the term, just know that it means we have to respect all our resources. Plastic is Mother Nature's nonrenewable resource, and time is ours. Let's not waste either one.

SELF–
CARE

DAYS

1 — 5

AIM FOR EFFORT, NOT PERFECTION

I clearly remember sitting at the edge of my bed when my daughter was six weeks old and the idea of being a "perfect" mother had fallen to pieces. My daughter wasn't sleeping, and neither was I. I was a shell of a person, trying everything and anything to make her sleep, desperately clutching at memories of my old life while trying to figure out my new role as a mother.

When the facade fell away (and when I finally got some sleep), I began to see that none of this was sustainable. I couldn't continue being the picture-perfect, twenty-first century, environmentally conscious woman while juggling all the demands of being a new mother. I learned my first hard lesson: that sustainability has to be sustainable for you.

That is why the first step in this thirty-day guide is acceptance that we should aim for effort, not perfection. To do this, we need to be nonjudgmental, toward others and particularly toward ourselves. Low-waste living does not mean you get to sit on a high horse.

We need to accept that we are all trying our goddamn best. Let's begin by loosening our grip on the "perfect" way to live a zero waste life and accept that making an effort in everything we do all adds up to a big cumulative difference. This might mean one night you're too tired to cook, so you order home delivery, but it might also mean you wash all the plastic packaging from the delivery and reuse it for your next freezer meals. Every effort made should be congratulated.

I want you to begin this thirty-day journey by writing a short manifesto on how to be a gentle activist. A gentle activist is one who is kind toward others and themselves about how much they can do and what they expect of others. You can return to this manifesto whenever everything seems too overwhelming or when you feel as if you're not doing enough.

Take three deep breaths. Write down what you want to get out of these thirty days. Here are some writing prompts.

I AM KIND TO MYSELF BECAUSE

_____

_____

I ACCEPT THINGS DON'T HAVE
TO BE PERFECT AND INSTEAD

_____

_____

I AM A GENTLE ACTIVIST BECAUSE

_____

_____

Here are some essential tips on how to be a gentle activist and a gentler parent.

2. **GO WITH THE FLOW** – As a parent, I've learned to be flexible and not to try to control the outcome. This mindset also applies to activism. It is important to be adaptable and flexible when adopting your zero waste lifestyle. Some days you'll be kicking butt, and other days you might be succumbing to plastic-wrapped snacks that your children are nagging you for. Don't beat yourself up about it. It is important to know that tomorrow is a new day, and you can always try again.

3. **EMBRACE THE "MOTHER" IN MOTHER EARTH** – Being a parent has made me so much more attuned to nature and the world around me. I think this is because I've come to realize how precious life is. Embrace the nurturing attitude that comes with being a parent, and use it to fuel the new habits you'll be adopting as a family.

4. **LEAD BY EXAMPLE** – Children are our most important mirrors; they reflect the best and the worst of us. Your actions should reflect your values and the values you want your children to adopt. Let's be conscious of how we set foot in this world and try to leave a gentler footprint.

5. **TEACH, DON'T PREACH** – In adopting a zero waste life, you may encounter some resistance. Instead of arguing or fighting about it, teach your children and family members the benefits of living zero waste and plastic free. Discuss the issues, such as plastic poisoning our sea life, or food waste contributing to climate change, and show them that they can make simple switches that require little to no effort. As the adage goes, you attract more flies with honey than vinegar. No one likes being preached to, but everyone likes being empowered to do good.

6. **MORE PLAY, FEWER CHORES** – Contrary to popular belief, living a zero waste life does not mean you spend all your free time doing chores and housework. It's simply about embracing new habits and getting the whole family involved. In fact, by living simply and embracing minimalism, you will find you have more time. This means more play, more laughter and more freedom!

CHOP WOOD, CARRY WATER

There is a Zen Buddhist story that goes a little like this. A young Buddhist monk asked his wise Zen master, "What does one do when one reaches enlightenment?" The Zen master replied, "What did you do this morning?" The young monk said, "Chop wood, carry water." The Zen master responded, "Before enlightenment, chop wood, carry water. After enlightenment, chop wood, carry water."

I love this story because it shows that there is no ideal state of "perfection" or "enlightenment," and that what you do every day is all part of the journey. In fact, what you do every day matters much more than what you do occasionally. It's these daily habits that you can achieve through effort, the cumulative effect of which matters more than trying to attain the perfect "zero" in zero waste living.

MINIMIZE YOUR DISTRACTIONS

Becoming a mother has given me "all the feels." It is the first time I have ever given myself entirely to another person, both literally and figuratively, and I have never been so scared in my life. Being a parent has been described as "watching your heart walk around outside your chest," and that is how I feel whenever I look at my daughter. I feel so much more in every way possible. Her tears are my tears, her anxieties are my own, her laughter is also my joy. This sense of feeling so much more has meant that my nerves are raw. I feel so much that I've become fearful. I look at the world around me, on constant alert for choking hazards and fall risks. I read the news with trepidation, scared of what the future will be like for my daughter. This parental anxiety has me wanting to wrap her in cotton wool and never let her leave the house.

All parents may experience these fears at one point or another. We live in a world with a twenty-four-hour news cycle, and advertising and social media constantly vying for our attention. This added noise makes us more anxious, more angry and more fearful.

Climate change is the most important issue the world faces. However, watching the news with a feverish obsession, or mindlessly scrolling through social media, isn't going to change anything. We need to have practical steps to break away from the noise so that we can get to work.

Today is the day to let go of these fears and become fearless. We need to be aware, but not scared. We need to educate our children, but not shock them. We need to be firm but gentle in our approach.

Here are my self-care tips to ensure you're fearless, not overwhelmed.

1. **READ LONG-FORM NEWS INSTEAD OF JUST THE HEADLINES** — Instead of watching the news on TV every day and scaring yourself silly before breakfast, subscribe to reputable news outlets and only allow news subscriptions to be sent to your inbox once a day or once a week rather than every hour or every day. Dedicate time to read and process these articles rather than skimming your way through sensationalist clickbait news headlines.

2. **LIMIT YOUR SOCIAL MEDIA EXPOSURE** — Don't use your phone for the first thirty minutes and last thirty minutes of the day. Avoiding screens for the first hour and last hour of the day is recommended—in the morning to prevent decision fatigue, and in the evening to give your brain enough downtime to prepare for sleep—but since we are all busy parents, thirty minutes is a good balance. To do this, you can set time limits on your apps, or simply put your phone away in another room. It is essential that you don't sleep with your phone next to you—the temptation is too close! If you use your phone as an alarm, consider investing in an old-fashioned alarm clock so you can put your phone out of arm's reach. Your sleep will thank you for it.

3. **MONOTASK, NOT MULTITASK** — Multitasking is *so* 1990s. It used to be the productivity buzzword but, thank goodness, we've moved on from that. Numerous studies have shown that multitasking means you spread yourself too thinly across tasks and end up doing nothing well. I am sure you've noticed that when you're on your phone replying to a work email, cooking dinner and trying to listen

to your child talking about their day, you end up doing none of those things properly and, in fact, it takes much longer than if you just did those things one by one. From today, try to concentrate on one task at a time. You and your children will be happier for it.

4. **STOP PLAYING SMALL** – Have you noticed we often "play small" by making ourselves conform to the people around us? We laugh along when someone makes fun of "greenies," when we secretly think we can all be better environmentalists. We ignore someone making an insensitive remark, because we don't want to make a fuss. I am guilty of both those things. But it's time to stop playing small and conforming to values that don't align with who you really are. It's okay to stand up for what you believe in, it's okay to be different and live a plastic-free life, and it's okay to disagree with people. It is time we grow up and become the adults that our children see us to be. Living in alignment with your values is the essence of what this thirty-day guide is about. It's about living your authentic truth: that you care about the environment, the state of the planet and what the future looks like for your children. By seeing you living your truth, your children will see you as a role model and be braver and more confident themselves. Even more importantly, you will be happier, because you're standing up for what you believe in.

THE "THREE STEPS TO ZERO WASTE" METHOD

A good illustration of how we can cut down on the "noise" of the modern world is to simplify the confusion about recycling. People say to me all the time, "I am a good environmentalist, I *recycle!*" Recycling is important, but in fact plastic is not so much recycled as it is *downcycled.* This means that, unlike glass, metal and cardboard, which can be recycled infinitely without degradation to the quality of the material, plastic is converted into poorer and poorer forms of plastic until it cannot be downcycled any further, at which point it sits in a landfill leaching greenhouse gases and contributing to climate change.

That's why plastic pollution is terrible for the planet. Explain this to your family and seek out alternatives that will work for you. This is where the "three steps to zero waste" method comes in. I designed it to allow flexibility and ease when embarking on a zero waste life. You can adapt these three steps to suit wherever you are on your journey.

STEP 1. REDUCE YOUR WASTE – This means using what you already have before buying anything new. It's the best method for people starting on their zero waste journey, because it avoids the consumption of virgin materials and prevents waste simply by using resources you already have.

STEP 2. LOW WASTE OPTION – This means using recyclable materials such as glass, paper, cardboard or metal products, which can be infinitely recycled without degradation to the quality of material. These products have a better long-term life cycle than plastic, which ultimately ends up in landfill.

STEP 3. ZERO WASTE OPTION – This means buying items that are package-free, and minimizing any form of waste. This could mean buying products "naked" or making your own.

CREATE A MORNING ROUTINE

Steve Jobs, Barack Obama and Ariana Huffington are all known for their morning routines. For them, starting their day on "autopilot" is necessary so that they can concentrate on making important decisions at work. Expending energy on deciding what cereal to eat for breakfast and what to wear would use up their decision-making muscle, resulting in unnecessary decision fatigue. While being a parent is not the same as running a nation or a billion-dollar company—it is harder! Creating a morning routine for yourself and your family allows everyone to start each day in a comfortable and predictable manner, making your lives easier and setting the tone for the day ahead.

A morning routine is also about *you*. It carves out time in the day to nourish yourself, even if it's just ten minutes. Before I had my daughter, I had a morning routine that was scheduled to the minute and allowed for an indulgent one-hour self-care routine consisting of journal writing, long meditations, tea ceremonies and yoga. Those days are long gone! My morning routine now, which I set out below, is a realistic model for parents with busy schedules and screaming kids. It's not an idealized, Instagram-worthy ritual espoused by tech entrepreneurs: it is something that sets good habits from the moment you wake up. A good morning routine provides a moment of calm before the storm of the day.

ESTABLISHING A MORNING ROUTINE

My routine is broken down into BC (before children wake up) and AC (after children wake up). However, getting a morning routine in place really starts the night before, and that means getting enough sleep. Here are my tips for a good night's sleep.

- **COUNT THE HOURS** – Most people require seven to nine hours of sleep per night for optimal functioning. Set an alarm for when you need to wake up and also when you need to get into bed. This will ensure you get an adequate amount of sleep every night.

- **WRITE IT DOWN** – Many people find they can't get to sleep because they are mentally occupied by ruminating over what happened during the day, or thinking about the tasks needing to be done tomorrow. The best way to clear your mind is to do a "mind dump" and write everything down in a notebook before you go to bed.

- **END THE DAY WITHOUT SCREENS** – The light emitted by our devices disrupts production of melatonin, the hormone that regulates sleep cycles. Try to have at least thirty minutes of screen-free time before bed. This ensures your brain understands it is time for sleep and gives your body time to produce melatonin. Also try to avoid loud music, violent TV programs and other forms of media that raise your adrenaline levels just before bed.

BEFORE CHILDREN WAKE UP (BC) – THE THREE 'S'S

Set your alarm for thirty minutes before your children wake up. This thirty minutes is your time. If you have younger children who wake up earlier, set it to fifteen minutes, or however much time you can allow yourself.

"You time" can be broken down into three essential components, which I recommend you approach in this order:

1. STRETCH – Hop straight out of bed, pyjamas and all, and stretch for five to ten minutes. Do some relaxing yoga stretches, such as sun salutations, or some other light movement—whatever gets you out of bed and moving in a gentle way. The point of this is to get your blood circulating, encouraging energy and movement for the day ahead. I like to follow the same YouTube video every morning until I've memorized it. This is not a time to make complex decisions: make sure you choose something you've done before, or choose a video before you go to sleep and bookmark it for when you wake.

   Some words of encouragement for those who don't enjoy exercise: this is not designed to be a vigorous workout, it is just meant to warm up your body and allow some time for yourself. It could be as simple as doing some stretches in bed—no need to change into exercise clothes, no need for any special techniques, just get moving. Even if exercising is something you love to do in the morning, for most parents getting to the gym can seem like an insurmountable task, as it requires you to get changed, get there, shower afterward and get back before the day begins for the rest of your family. By doing five to ten minutes of gentle movement, you're encouraging positive habits to form. This "bite-sized" movement activity is a great way to transform your exercise habits for the long term.

2. **STILLNESS** – Meditate, sit in stillness or sit quietly in your bed— whatever you decide, this is a time for quiet reflection. Don't overcomplicate it. Whatever type of meditation or mindfulness you want to practice, just be sure to do it for five to fifteen minutes a day. I used to be a skeptic about the benefits of meditation, but it has been a life-changing practice for me. It provides an anchor in the chaos of life. Don't just take my word for it, however; numerous studies have shown that meditation in any form reduces stress and increases performance throughout the day.

Make meditation a part of your daily mental fitness regime. As a society we spend so much time focused on physical fitness while often neglecting to do the same for our brains. Let's flex those mind muscles and make meditation a daily habit. If you're new to meditation, you could try using a guided meditation app such as Calm, Smiling Mind or Headspace. If you're an old pro, this is a reminder to ensure it is a daily nonnegotiable.

3. **SELF-NOURISHMENT** – The final part of the BC morning routine consists of self-nourishment. This means reading an uplifting or empowering book for five to ten minutes. For some, this might mean reading a religious text; for others it might mean reading some poetry or an inspiring memoir. You can also enjoy an insightful audiobook or podcast if you prefer.

Before I had my daughter, I was a prolific reader. I loved reading autobiographies of inspirational leaders, and I immersed myself in poetry and classical texts. Reading fell by the wayside when I became a mother. At the end of the day, I was too exhausted to digest anything heavy and my memory span became like that of a goldfish. Reading for five to ten minutes in the morning is something that is achievable and also nourishes your mind and soul. As a parent, it can be easy to forget that you're a mature, intelligent individual who has interests besides the Wiggles's entire back catalog. This small nugget of time is a precious reminder that you deserve a daily opportunity to feed your mind and soul.

MY FAVORITE BOOKS FOR EARLY-MORNING READING

Devotions by Mary Oliver – I love this anthology of poems. I often pick up the book and turn to a random page. It's always a magical experience, and her words always speak to my soul.

The Daily Stoic by Ryan Holiday and Stephen Hanselman – This is a book of daily insights based on the works of the Stoic philosophers. It covers resilience, strength and wisdom, quoting from ancient Greeks and Romans who ruled expansive empires, fought endless wars and managed political backstabbers on a daily basis. If they can't give us advice on how to live, no one can.

Tao Te Ching (The Way) by Laozi – This is a wonderful book with many different translations. Once again, it is a book that you can open to any page and find some beautiful insight about what it means to be human. I love the simplicity of the text, which is elegant in its own right, but it gives way to deeper nuance the more you contemplate it.

AFTER CHILDREN WAKE UP
(AC) – THE THREE 'C's

1. **COMFORT** – When the children wake up, always start the day with words or actions of comfort. For little ones, a hug and kiss and a quick snuggle in bed is often enough. For older kids, a happy greeting and a chat about what dreams they had or what they are looking forward to that day is a simple way to show that they are loved.

   I grew up in an emotionally closed-off family, and my parents were not ones to show their affection outwardly. I rarely remember my parents saying good morning or greeting me with a smile—it was just not the "done thing" in my household. I vowed to change that when I had my own children. Waking up to comfort in the form of a simple smile and hug provides warmth and love, and is a reminder to a child that every day is a good day.

2. **CARE** – Do things with intention and care. Instead of spending the time making too many new decisions, make the morning routine seamless. Have a capsule wardrobe for your children (more about this later) and prepare simple breakfasts that are predictable, nutritious and easy to make (more about this later too). The fewer decisions you have to make in the morning about how to care for your child, the fewer arguments there will be about what to eat and what to wear. Make the morning an autopilot process for all, so that you aren't worn out before you even get to work or go to school.

3. **CALM** – Turn off all noise in the morning. This means no radio, TV or social media. Ask your children to start the day peacefully, without any distractions. Wash, eat and get ready in silence and enjoy some calm as a family before the world rushes in.

"MINI-TATION" – MEDITATION FOR CHILDREN

From around the age of five, children can begin to learn to meditate or sit in stillness. It is recommended that you give them a mantra or a word that they can repeat in their minds to help them focus. Choose a word that doesn't have any connotations or associations, or just a sound, like "ohm." Ask them to repeat this sound in their mind, gently, like the light touch of a feather or a caress. As a starting point, children can aim to meditate for as many minutes as they are years old: a five-year-old can aim for five minutes, a seventeen-year-old for seventeen minutes.

LESS, BUT BETTER

One of the questions I get asked most frequently is, "How do you do it all?" The answer is, I don't do it all *at once*. Parents are constantly toggling between different open browser tabs. We are cleaning, driving, singing, soothing, working, teaching, and often all at once. However, this constant overload of tasks can inevitably lead your brain to "unexpectedly quit" and your body to undergo a complete shutdown. Burnout is a common side effect of overwhelm.

Minimalism is a concept that I want you to embrace. My definition of minimalism does not involve white, angular homes with turtleneck-wearing inhabitants; it involves doing less, and being better. We all need to *do* less—not *be* less, just do less—so that we can all feel better. Today I challenge you to consolidate your schedule and the tasks you have to complete.

In societies around the world, we are overscheduling our children from a young age. We are training them to be Olympic athletes and the next child prodigies in arts, sciences and music. At only one year old, my daughter had more social engagements than I did! We all know the standard Saturday routine: sport in the morning, a birthday party at midday, music or language lessons in the afternoon and, of course, a sleepover at night. You spend the whole day chauffeuring, cooking and entertaining, and by the end of the day, everyone is exhausted. Sunday is another hamster-wheel of a day and, by the end of the weekend, you need another weekend to recover!

Start embracing the "less, but better" motto by asking yourself these questions:

1. What can I cut from the schedule today?
2. Do my children actually enjoy doing so many extracurricular activities?
3. When is the scheduled "downtime" for me and the children?
4. Is there a good reason for everything in this schedule? If not, why is it there?

These are confronting questions to ask yourself. Why are we overscheduling ourselves to the brink of exhaustion? What are we trying to prove to ourselves and others by signing up our children to endless sports clubs, music lessons, academic tutoring and events with friends and extended family? I believe we all start off with the best intentions. We want our children to succeed in life and be happy. We think that signing them up to cello lessons, hockey games, math tutoring and all the birthday parties will help them become bright, talented, social individuals. But, in reality, it will just make them (and you) exhausted. The greatest gift you can give your children is your time, guidance and attention. No number of extracurricular activities can replace active and mindful parenting. Let's put the calendars away, and focus on what's really important: time with your children.

"LESS, BUT BETTER" – THE THREE QUESTIONS

To apply the "less, but better" rule, we can start by minimizing our day-to-day schedules. I want you to examine your week and focus on all the events and activities that you and your children have signed up for. Start with your own schedule and ask yourself the following three questions:

1. DOES DOING THIS ACTIVITY FEEL "HEAVY" OR "LIGHT"?

An activity that feels "heavy" is one that you dread all week long, and when you're there, you can't wait for it to be over. "Light" activities are the opposite: you look forward to them, relish them and can't wait to do them all again. If it feels heavy, let it go. Life is too short. If going to coffee with your mother-in-law every week feels heavy, politely drop it from your schedule. Find another activity and timeslot that accommodates your schedule. If your children hate hockey, let it go. Find activities for yourself and your family that make you feel light and joyous. Involve your children in this process and ask them this question for each of their activities. Children will be brutally honest with you—and you'll all be happier for it.

2. WHO AM I DOING THIS FOR?

We often find ourselves doing things because "we have to." Remember, you're an adult with judgment and free will; no one can force you to do anything you don't want to do. If you don't want to attend your workplace's weekly after-hours networking drinks, you don't have to. If you don't want to go to Uncle John's wedding in Bali, you don't have to. You can politely refuse any engagements you don't want to attend. There are a host of real and honest reasons why you can refuse all these activities, even though they seem like necessary engagements. Tell your boss that you'll need to organize after-hours childcare to be able to attend drinks. Tell Uncle John that it's not within your budget to go to Bali at the moment because you are saving for a family vacation, but you would love to catch up with him after his wedding. Give yourself the permission to say no to things that don't light you up, and say *yes* to life instead.

3. WILL DOING THIS ACTIVITY ALLOW ME ENOUGH TIME TO REST?

We live in a world in which our time is measured by our productivity, but there is no metric for measuring the value of downtime. When I worked in aerospace engineering, we regularly scheduled "downtime" for our aircrafts so that they could be maintained, fixed and restored. Why aren't we scheduling in downtime for humans? Numerous studies have shown the importance of sleep and rest to allow for cell regeneration and brain recuperation. Without rest, we simply aren't capable of functioning at optimal levels. We need to start scheduling downtime in our busy lives, and our children's lives. As a general rule, for every activity scheduled I also schedule in downtime before and after the event. This "buffer zone" ensures adequate time for the whole family to prepare for the activity, enjoy the activity and rest afterward.

THE BINARY
BAROMETER

Since adopting a more minimalist mindset, I've applied the "less, but better" principle to all aspects of my life, including clothing, furniture, activities and even friendships. The "less, but better" principle allows you to reflect on your values. It brings into focus the things that light you up and the things that you need to remove from your life.

You can judge this by gauging your reaction when you ask yourself, *Does this feel heavy or light?*

If you clench your stomach, grind your teeth and feel a sense of dread, it's time to let that item or activity go. If it feels easy, gentle, joyful and light-filled, it is something you enjoy and maybe should try to accommodate even more of. This binary barometer is an exercise that allows you to monitor your own emotions and reactions to items, activities and people in your life. At first, your barometer might not be so binary. However, if you practice this exercise consistently, over time you'll know instantly what will fill you with joy.

SHARE THE LOAD

Someone recently asked me, "What is the biggest change you've experienced as a mother?" and I replied, "It's the most alone I've ever felt." Even though I was always with people, my daughter or others, I felt entirely alone. Parenthood is incredibly joyous and the most nourishing thing I've ever done, but it's also the loneliest. The feeling of isolation comes from the long, sleepless nights, the frustration you feel when you can't soothe your child's cries, and the sense that you are never doing enough and will never make everyone happy.

There are also some hard facts about being a new mother that no one ever told me. The seclusion of breastfeeding, for example: you are often hidden away in another room with your child or, even worse, if you're pumping breastmilk at work then you're hidden away in some dark, forsaken corner of the workplace, spending your precious break time in social isolation. There is also the anxiety you feel about having to make decisions that will affect another person's life without any real reassurance that what you are doing will be right for them in the long run. It's scary how scary parenting can be!

The best thing I did after becoming a mother was to talk to my parents and to other parents. If you don't attend a parents' group, make your own informal one and, no matter how busy life gets, make time for it. It's a lifeline to get you out of your well of loneliness. It's also a great way to ask for help. You can ask for practical things, such as asking someone to watch your child because you haven't been to the bathroom all day, but it's also a way to seek assistance in more indirect ways. It's an outlet for you to ask, "I don't know what I am doing, do you?" As the adage goes, it takes a village to raise a child. We all need to create our own villages to share the physical and emotional load.

Today is a day to ask for help. In asking for help, we are reducing our workload and learning to rely on others, not just ourselves. We are learning to not waste time on small tasks but instead to save it for the things that matter most. Most of us know when we have to ask for help, but often we don't actually know what we need help with. Here are some practical tips about how to ask for help that will improve your life, and what form that help might take.

1. **OUTSOURCE YOUR CHORES** – Can you outsource some of the housework? If it's within your means, why not pay for a cleaner once a fortnight or once a month, or perhaps pay someone to maintain your garden regularly? A simple way to do this that benefits both you and your community is to ask your friends and family if they know of anyone who is looking to make some extra money. Often teenagers, university students or people looking to subsidize their income would be glad to form a mutually beneficial arrangement. You can ask for referrals from Facebook, post a notice at the local library or even join a local parents' group, to ask for advice.

2. **GET THINGS DELIVERED** – Living a zero waste life will require you to make some changes, and this is one that will make your life so much easier! I no longer have time to go to farmers' markets every week: instead, I choose to get an organic fruit and vegetable box delivered to me once a fortnight. This saves time and money and, most importantly, it also reduces plastic waste. When you are getting items delivered from a local seller, you are contributing to a system that helps farmers and small businesses. Not only are you saving yourself time, money and fuel that would be used driving to the shops every week, you are contributing directly to farmers and small businesses by voting with your dollar. The company I choose delivers everything in a cardboard box, which they take back to be reused when it is empty, and all the produce is "naked," meaning there's no plastic packaging. It's also extremely cost effective because the farmers choose in-season produce for you and you eliminate the middleman taking their cut. This has been such

a game-changer for my family—we always have fresh, organic food without my ever having to go to the supermarket.

3. ASK FOR "VOUCHERS" OF TIME AS GIFTS – When it comes to milestones and events, instead of receiving more "stuff," why not ask your loved ones for gifts of time? Ask if people can make you some home-cooked meals, babysit for a couple of hours, take your children out to see a movie or even mow your lawn. These can be given as "vouchers" that can be redeemed as gifts for birthdays, Christmas presents or baby shower gifts. The gift of time is the best gift of all.

4. VOICE YOUR CONCERNS – As the saying goes, a problem shared is a problem halved. Sometimes we don't need any actual solutions or quick fixes, we just need someone to listen. That's why talking to other parents is essential for your own well-being. Whenever I feel overwhelmed, I pick up the phone and call a friend. If they are busy, I might leave them a lengthy message to share my thoughts and vent my frustrations. You can even start the phone call with, "I am just calling to vent, there's no need to try to fix anything, I would just appreciate someone listening." By physically voicing your concerns and getting things off your chest, you will feel better. Vocalizing something that you've been stewing over can make the problem seem much less significant. And remember, if you feel like you need an outside opinion or if you don't feel you can reach out to your friends, there are also free advice services open to you. Search the internet for a parent helpline in your area.

5. SEEK SOME ALONE TIME – Contrary to what you might think,

alone time won't make you feel more lonely. Scheduling time for yourself is a form of self-care. It's so important to set aside time to do something for you, without anyone else around. This might mean asking your partner to look after the children every Saturday morning, or even paying for a babysitter once every fortnight so you can both get some respite. Having some quality time to yourself is an important part of being a good caregiver. Here are some restorative ideas for you to schedule in.

- Do some yoga or light exercise.
- Go for a run or walk along the beach.
- Catch the train to a new destination and spend a few hours being a tourist.
- Go for a swim in a scenic outdoor pool.
- Sit in a café or bar and have a drink by yourself.
- Go to a film festival and enjoy a film by yourself.
- Sit in a café and read a book just for pleasure.
- Scour a weekend market for some secondhand finds.
- Go for a long hike and listen to an audiobook or podcast.
- Go to an art gallery and wander wherever your eye takes you.
- Go to a matinee performance of an opera, ballet or theater production.

Most of these things don't cost a lot of money, nor do they take up a lot of time, but I guarantee if you regularly schedule in some "you" time, the whole household will feel better for it.

ASKING FOR HELP – THE NEW SUPERPOWER

Raising a family is not a test of endurance. It is not a test of your character or strength. Don't be afraid to ask for help. You'll be surprised by how many people will gladly put up their hands to help if you just ask. You can ask for help minding the children, doing grocery shopping, doing school pick-ups. If your children are too young to be left alone with strangers, then ask for help around the home. If your children are older, ask them to help you. Being a parent doesn't have to be a lonely task. You are not weak if you ask for help; in fact, learning to do so is a superpower!

HOME
CARE

DAYS

6 - 15

CREATE A COMMAND STATION

In my career as an aerospace engineer, I learned that the most important part of any mission is the command station. Apollo 11 would have been nothing without Houston. Today is the day to create your own "Houston" for your home. This is the central message board that organizes your home life and ensures everyone is engaged in the zero waste lifestyle.

It is important that your command station is visually appealing and displayed in a high-traffic area of your home. My command station is a whiteboard on my fridge. Additional documents are neatly arranged around the board with magnets. There is nothing else on my fridge except the command station and documents. You can use a bulletin board in your front entranceway or a dedicated wall space with colored Post-it notes: the key is to make it easily accessible and highly visible. To supplement this command station, I also have a shared cloud storage drive with my husband so that we both have access to digital copies of important documents and bills. As your children get older, you can consider making your command station digital with a shared document. For now, it is important that your command station is centralized, and becomes the control center for all household activities.

It is also important to do a quick review of the command station once a week. I plan "family meetings" for half an hour on a Saturday morning to discuss the components of the command station and update them as necessary. Family meetings are so important, and have really changed the trajectory of my family's well-being. In our work lives we regularly schedule meetings for group projects and to make sure everyone's on track to meet deadlines. We need to start applying some of those principles at home to make everyone's lives a little easier. It is also essential to hold family meetings to make sure everyone is engaged and on board with any changes that occur when adopting a zero waste life.

CREATING YOUR "HOUSTON"

There are four essential components to my family command station: the family contract, household schedule, shopping list and general notes.

FAMILY CONTRACT

These are agreed rules that are cosigned by all family members. If you have young children, the family contract can be discussed verbally, and pictures can be used to represent the rules. The family contract outlines house rules and helps educate your children on the reasons for the lifestyle changes you may be embarking on. A general principle for the family contract is to keep it simple: a maximum of five rules is more than enough.

Examples of the kinds of rules you could include are:

1. **RESPECT EACH OTHER AND RESPECT THE PLANET** – This creates an opportunity to discuss with your family the importance of being caretakers for the planet and why you are embarking on a zero waste life.

2. **TRY YOUR BEST AT ALL TIMES** – This allows for an open discussion about making an effort in schoolwork, home life and your new zero waste habits.

3. **BE HONEST WITH EACH OTHER** – This involves promoting integrity and honesty in all areas of your lives. It also gives each family member the opportunity to openly discuss their concerns about any lifestyle change.

4. **DO YOUR PART** – This ensures everyone contributes to the household, whether by doing chores and helping others out or by holding each other accountable for adopting new habits.

5. **HAVE FUN!** – Always end with a positive rule. Remember, embarking on a zero waste life means more money, time and freedom for you to do things you really love as a family. It's not about deprivation, it's about making time for things that matter and living in alignment with your values.

HOUSEHOLD SCHEDULE

I have a schedule on the whiteboard that outlines each family member's activities for the week. It also includes chores, shopping days and other family activities. This ensures everyone knows what they are doing when.

ACTIVITIES

In *Day 4: Less, but better*, we discussed applying the principles of minimalism to our personal schedules and the family schedule. It is now important that we put those principles into action and outline the schedule for the whole family in the command station. Don't forget to double-check there is enough buffer time around activities and schedule in rest periods too.

CHORES

Children as young as five years old can start helping around the house. Giving them simple chores and sharing responsibility for the upkeep of the home allows them an insight into the complexities of running a household. For young children, tidying up their toys, taking their dishes to the sink, wiping benchtops and play areas, and sorting laundry are helpful tasks that empower them to take charge of their own housekeeping. For older children, chores such as cooking, sorting recycling or maintaining the compost or worm farm allow them to get their hands dirty. Don't think of chores as a burden we're placing on our kids: they are a way for parents to empower children to become independent and self-sufficient.

ADMIN

On the household schedule, make sure you put in any "admin" tasks such as upcoming family meetings and grocery shopping trips. This might also include a list of errands such as visits to the bank, pharmacy and gardening store. This allows you to better plan for these errands to ensure you don't need multiple trips to the same location.

SHOPPING LIST

On the command station, a section should be dedicated to a shopping list. Knowing what is in your pantry and having a running inventory allows you to prevent food waste. If you only buy food when you have run out, you will prevent yourself from shopping irrationally and buying extra of things you already have. I used to be guilty of this myself: buying bags of pasta when I already had four at home, or buying cans of chickpeas because they were on sale when there were still cans in the pantry from the last sale. A centralized shopping list is critical to figuring out what is really needed at the next bulk shopping, farmers' market or supermarket trip.

GENERAL NOTES

The command station should have a general notes section to include miscellaneous items such as forms that need to be signed, bills that need to be paid, appointments that need to be booked. It's also a nice idea to put an interesting news article for people to read, a quick note of thanks or an inspirational quote in this section. Just because a command station is practical doesn't mean it can't be fun too!

THE TRASH
COMMAND STATION

Today is also an important day to set up the trash command station. In my home I divide my trash into DRY TRASH, which is sorted into three pedal-press bins, and WET TRASH, which is sorted into compost and bokashi (fermenting) containers. All these bins and containers are clearly labeled to ensure everyone knows where everything should go.

DRY TRASH

1. RECYCLING BIN — It's important to check with your local council what can actually be recycled, as it differs from council to council. They will usually have a one-page information sheet that you can tape onto the lid of your bin.

2. SOFT PLASTICS BIN — Soft plastic (i.e. any plastic that is scrunchable) can be recycled! You can find soft plastic recycling collection points outside many major supermarkets. Keep a separate bin for this, so that you can take your soft plastics to be recycled on a regular basis.

3. LANDFILL – This bin is clearly labeled "landfill" as a reminder to all household members where any trash they put in this bin ends up. We talk about throwing something "away," but there is no such thing as "away"—it ends up in a landfill, producing methane gas, which is a significant contributor to global warming.

WET TRASH

1. COMPOST BIN – This includes all fruit and vegetable scraps. I have a kitchen benchtop container that I put my scraps into. You can dispose of this into your compost bin whenever it's full. If you don't have a compost bin at home, you can put it in the fridge or freezer and take it to a community compost bin once a week, or even dispose of it in a friend's compost bin when you visit them.

The internet is a great resource for finding community compost bins. In some neighborhoods, community members even note in community groups whether they are willing to allow their neighbors to add to their compost.

2. BOKASHI BIN (FERMENTING BIN) – I have a separate container in my freezer where I freeze all animal products such as bones and shells. Once a fortnight, I take these out of the freezer and put them into my bokashi bin. This is a natural fertilizing bin with a tap at the base of the bin. The bokashi system works to ferment food scraps and animal products into a powerful liquid fertilizer that you can pour onto your plants. Once a year, you need to bury the solid waste from this bin in soil. You can also compost this solid waste in your compost bin.

Do your own research about which system will work for you: some people have chickens, worm farms or other creative solutions to deal with their wet trash. There are options to suit all sorts of different lifestyles and living arrangements. It's all about creating a trash command station that works for you!

TO DO

MAKE A HOME FOR ALL YOUR BELONGINGS

Before I had my daughter, I went to visit a friend who had two young children. Their house was filled to the brim with toys, there were mountains of clothing everywhere and everything seemed to be on the brink of bedlam. I thought to myself, *When I have kids, this will not be me.* Fast forward two years and my small apartment was filled to the brim with toys, there were mountains of washing everywhere and everything seemed on the brink of bedlam. I've come to accept that chaos is part of being a parent. *Temporary* chaos is a perfectly acceptable thing. You can't live in a picture-perfect home, because your children will be there doing what kids do: creating mess and having fun. The solution is to surrender to this chaos *temporarily*, and ensure that everything is returned to where it belongs at the end of the day.

Today is a day to declutter and make sure everything in your home has a home. In *A Zero Waste Life*, I run through a three-day decluttering challenge designed to minimize your possessions in a systematic way, which you can follow if you are looking to do a major overhaul. But a simple rule for decluttering is that everything must have a place where it belongs, and if it doesn't have a home, then you must responsibly get rid of it. If you embrace "everything must have a home" as a guiding principle, I guarantee that tidying your home at the end of the day will take no longer than five to ten minutes.

Remember, your external environment influences your internal environment. If your home is chaotic, how can you expect your children to thrive? Most people want belonging, not more belongings.

Let's begin by discussing some practical guidelines for a tidy, decluttered home.

1. **USE WHAT YOU HAVE** – Don't be tempted to buy anything new in terms of storage solutions until you've made a home for all your existing items. Deciding where your possessions will be kept automatically helps you define the boundaries you need to work within. For example:

    - **TOYS** – My daughter has two large baskets that all her toys must fit into. If the baskets start to overflow, it's time to do some decluttering and donate the extra toys. This is an important process to explain to your children. Don't throw things away without their permission—let them guide you on what should be kept or donated.

    - **CLOTHING** – My wardrobe consists of two dressers and a full-length wardrobe. All my clothing and accessories must be able to fit into these, and if I run out of space, it's time to declutter and responsibly donate clothing. This effectively means that if I bring anything new into my home, then I must make room for it by getting rid of something that I already own. Applying this "one in, one out" rule ensures that I am sensible with my purchases and I don't overconsume.

    - **BOOKS AND TRINKETS** – I have one display bookshelf for all the lovely books and ceramics that I have collected over the years. This shelf is the only place where I store my most prized possessions. This prevents me from collecting trinkets for the sake of collecting, and ensures my home doesn't become a dust magnet full of bric-a-brac. Many people have storage issues related to books: you could try opting for an e-reader, or borrowing books from the library. If you do love hard copies of books, don't deprive yourself, but do set a physical boundary, such as a dedicated set of bookshelves, to prevent the hoarding of books.

2. **DON'T STORE ANYTHING UNDER YOUR BED** – This is a general rule for not letting your house become a storage facility. In feng shui, having things underneath your bed is said to attract bad luck. If you're keeping things stored away, do you really need them?

   I once helped a friend who was suffering from asthma symptoms to declutter and organize her room. The first thing I did was look under her bed. It was packed full of miscellaneous items, and home to a colony of dust bunnies. We took everything out, donated the unwanted goods and found new homes for things she wanted to keep. We gave it a good vacuum and then left the area under the bed clear. She rang me the next day, overjoyed that her asthma symptoms had subsided, but also that she had received a phone call about a job she had interviewed for months earlier. She had given up on hearing back from them, but they had just called to say they wanted to work with her. She told me her luck had changed, all because she cleaned underneath her bed!

3. **CURATE YOUR HOME LIKE A MUSEUM** – Before you bring anything into your home, you should ask yourself the question,

"Where will I put it?" Ask your children to do the same. This is a great deterrent to excessive consumption and is a good reminder to make do with what you have. Giving all your items a home allows you to appreciate everything you own. Think of yourself as a museum curator: you should put the same level of effort and care into your home as a curator puts into their collection. Each piece should have breathing room, so that it can be enjoyed by everyone to its full capacity. Embrace this idea, and start removing the excess from your home.

4. **THE TEN-MINUTE TIDY** – Because everything in your home now has its own place to call home, your household tidy at the end of the day should take no more than ten minutes. At first this may seem impossible, but trust me, after some careful curation, and making space for everything within the confines of the storage solutions you already have, tidying will be a breeze! At the end of the day, I set a quick ten-minute timer and return all the toys, books, cups, plates and miscellaneous items to their respective homes. The ten-minute timer makes the task seem more manageable. At the end of a long day, tidying might seem like a mammoth task, but by setting yourself a timer you will realize it's a task with an end in sight, and quite often, you won't even need the whole ten minutes! As your children get older, they can join in the ten-minute tidy. Once everything has a home, tidying is no longer stressful, and chaos is only ever temporary.

MAKE DO WITH WHAT YOU HAVE

When embarking on a new lifestyle, it is tempting to buy shiny new things to suit that lifestyle. With zero waste living, you might feel the urge to run out and buy brand-new glass jars, stainless steel containers and other zero waste paraphernalia, which would defeat the purpose of living a zero waste life. The most eco-friendly solution is to make do with what you have. This means using what you already have, repairing, upcycling and mending items, and only buying something if you really need it.

Here are three uses for the humble glass jar:

1. Wrap a cloth napkin around it, secured with an elastic band, to make your own reusable coffee cup. You can also choose to decorate it with a layer of colored elastic bands to make a sleeve for your cup.

2. Use it to store your snacks or food for school or work. Small jars are handy for nuts and fruit pieces; large jars are good for salads, pasta and noodles. You can also use a clean jar to take home leftovers when you eat out.

3. Use it to give homemade gifts. You can make your own body scrub using 2 parts granulated sugar to 1 part olive oil and decant it into upcycled jars. You can also make other homemade gifts such as body moisturizers and bath salts.

A ZERO WASTE LIFE

MINIMALIST ROUTINES

Before I began living a more minimalist and zero waste lifestyle, I was the type of person who had an entire spare bedroom that I used as a storage room. It was my shameful little secret. Whenever I had guests over, I would just put everything in the spare room and close the door. That was my version of tidying up.

Looking back, I cringe at the thought of how much "stuff" was in my home. I was living a life of excess, crowding my home with more clothes, shoes and handbags, trying to fill a void that could not be sated by material goods. Living a truly zero waste life allowed me to determine the root cause of my shopping addiction, but this didn't happen overnight. It started with changing small, everyday habits, and now I am a new woman.

Start making small changes in your home by embracing some simple minimalist routines for you and your whole family. These changes may seem insignificant, but small, consistent effort is the key to making long-lasting change.

MAKE YOUR BED

Today is a day to instill new habits in your life, and we are starting with making your bed. Most of us overdecorate when it comes to our homes, and our beds are no exception—we have six throw pillows, two types of blankets and a throw rug on top. We want to make our homes look like the "after" in a reality TV renovation show, but in reality all this extra stuff is hard to maintain and we end up only making our beds when guests come over. As a parent, you don't have time to maintain a picture-perfect bedroom. The first rule is to keep it simple and do it every day. This goes for your children's beds as well. A made bed instantly makes a room look neater, and lifts the mood—quite simply, making your bed in the morning sets the tone for the day. You need to lead by example, and then show your children how to make their own beds. If you use a version of the minimalist bedding outlined here, even young children can make their beds and start the day right.

MINIMALIST
BEDDING

Here is a minimalist hack for you: reduce your bedding so it becomes easier to make your bed every morning. On my bed I have:

- AN OVERSIZED DUVET – This is a good trick to make everything look tidy without needing hospital corners. Opt for a duvet one size up from the size of your bed, so if you have a queen mattress you'll want a king-sized duvet. I just throw this duvet over my sheets and pillow every morning and my bed instantly looks neater.

- TWO PILLOWS – This is all I need for two people. The pillows are covered by the oversized duvet when the bed is made.

- TWO EUROPEAN (SQUARE) PILLOWS – These are placed on top of the duvet to create a point of interest. They also provide comfort when I'm sitting up in bed, because I don't have a headboard.

- WHITE BEDDING – Everything is in white linen to create a comfortable yet luxurious feel.

And that's it! You can do the same for your children's bedding as well. I made an investment by purchasing quality bedding and it has withstood the test of time. If you can't afford brand new linen sheets, try sourcing them secondhand or just buy the best quality you can afford. Remember, we spend a third of our lives in bed, so it's worth investing in our sleep.

REMOVE YOUR SHOES

In many Asian households, it is important to remove your shoes before you enter a home. There are hygiene reasons associated with this: it prevents outside dirt from entering the home, which is especially important if you have young children, and it also decreases the amount of cleaning you have to do. Aside from these practical reasons, removing your shoes is a sign of respect, not only to your host but also to their home. It's a symbolic gesture that says, "I am humbly entering your space." Ask your family members and guests to remove their shoes before they enter your home. I like to go barefoot once I am home, and in winter I wear thick woolen socks, but many people have indoor shoes such as slippers. Invest in some quality indoor footwear that is suitable for your family. Instill this new habit and make your life easier when it comes to cleaning. It can also become a small ritual at the end of the day, a signal that whatever happened *outside* today can be shed as you enter your home and sanctuary.

Making your bed and removing your shoes might seem to be inconsequential changes, but they are a representation of how small steps can make a big cumulative difference. Since I began my zero waste journey, many people have asked me, "How do I get my partner/family members/friends to live a more eco-friendly lifestyle?" The answer is to lead by example. As with any new habit, we need to embody the changes to show others that living a more eco-conscious life is not about sacrifice and deprivation; it's about making sensible swaps and making positive behaviors become habitual.

TEACH, DON'T PREACH

When you are embarking on changes in your life, it's understandable that you will be enthusiastic and will want to share your newfound perspective with everyone. However, we need to remind ourselves that not everybody is ready for change, and no one is ready for judgment. It's time for us to teach, not preach.

In my own zero waste journey, I've seen so many people sit on their high horses, judging others who aren't as zero waste as they are. I am sure I've done it myself from time to time. But I've come to realize this does nothing to help spread the message of zero waste living. We have to understand that we are all at different stages of change. It's okay to start small, and we don't need to do it all. We do need to show compassion for others, because we are all juggling different hardships. Let's all teach with grace.

I like teaching this simple motto: do what you can, when you can. An example of this is, when I can, I do my best to bring all my containers to the bulk store and buy all my groceries package-free. When life gets busy, or I forget my reusable containers, I might use the paper bags that are provided in-store. And if life is overwhelming, everything falls by the wayside and I end up buying plastic packaged goods at the supermarket, then pick myself up and try to do better the next time. This might involve creating a reminder system for myself before I go grocery shopping, or leaving some extra containers in the car. By teaching others this gentle way of thinking about zero waste living, I find there's less resistance, and more willingness to give it a go.

As well as this, we must also be conscious to only teach when asked. There's no need to lecture someone about your lifestyle if they haven't asked about it. The best way to influence others is to lead by example. Nowadays, I only tell people about my zero waste lifestyle when they ask. When people see my cloth napkin or reusable coffee cup and are genuinely curious about my way of life, I am happy to share tips. There's no need to preach to those who don't want to listen. When people see you are living a happy and carefree life, they will ask what your secret is, and you can share it with them then.

It's time to stop judging others and start living. We need more teachers in this world, not more preachers.

ZERO WASTE FOOD

When embarking on a zero waste lifestyle, many of the changes you'll make are centered on food. Since becoming a parent, I've come to understand firsthand how important it is to be able to make simple, easy, nutritious and delicious meals in the blink of an eye. It seems that everyone in the household is always hungry!

Until I was four years old, I lived with my grandmother in China while my parents emigrated to Australia to forge a new life for us. My grandmother's kitchen was incredibly humble, just a sink and a gas stove with a large wok. We lived in the heart of Guangzhou, and we were the only ones in our street with indoor plumbing. The rituals I remember all revolved around eating: the washing of rice, the peeling of vegetables, shopping for groceries in the street markets. My grandmother couldn't read or write, but she had a special skill in ensuring there was always food for everyone in the household. My mother tells stories of growing up in China in the 1960s, when meat was mainly eaten during Chinese New Year as a celebration, and otherwise only consumed in very small portions each month. Food is an important part of my life today because I have known what it is like to have little, and I've also known excess.

If you are reading this book, it is likely you are living in the developed world, where excess is a problem rather than deficiency. It is therefore our duty to be responsible food advocates, because there are so many people in the world who still live with less.

Teaching your children about where food comes from is an important first step in showing them all the resources that are required to bring a meal to your table. When you are wasting food, it isn't just the piece of broccoli that you're sending to a landfill: the labor used to grow the food, the energy used to harvest it, the resources used in transporting it, the hard-earned money used to buy it and the time and effort taken to cook it before it arrives on your dinner plate are all wasted too. Let's stop wasting food today.

THE TRUE
COST OF FOOD

An activity that you can do during a meal is to ask your children to examine every piece of food on their plate, and then ask them, "Where does your food come from? How did it get here? How is it made?" and other follow-up questions suited to their age. How much do we know about the food we eat?

A great example is rice. Rice seems like such an ordinary staple, yet it has some of the most backbreaking and labor-intensive growing and harvesting processes. Rice is sown in paddy fields and requires a constant water source. It is rarely grown with industrial machines, but rather mostly hand-grown by men and women bending over in fields ploughed by oxen. It is also harvested by hand and then stored in large silos to dry out the grains. Rice is mainly grown in Southeast Asia and India, and then transported around the world, eventually making its way to your dinner plate. Rice is also one of the foods that we most frequently throw away. If we measured more than just the financial cost of rice, and also considered the environmental, labor and energy costs of producing the food we eat, we wouldn't waste it so readily.

Explaining this to your children and getting them to do their own research—there are some excellent short YouTube videos about where food comes from, for example—is a great way to get them thinking about food and food waste. It helps children (and adults!) understand deeper questions about the true cost of what we eat, and this will cultivate an appreciation of food. This appreciation might encourage them to try more new foods and, most importantly, it will prevent food waste!

Here are some simple ideas to prevent food waste in the home. In *Day 10: Zero waste kitchen*, we will dive deeper and discuss how to organize your kitchen to prevent food waste.

MEAL PREP, NOT JUST MEAL PLAN

My first tip is to meal prep. Many people think that doing a weekly or monthly meal plan means less food waste and allows you to plan your shopping better. In reality, meal planning doesn't allow much flexibility and often locks you into meals. I find that meal prepping is a better way to think about it. Once my fruit and vegetable delivery box arrives, I spend thirty minutes washing and cutting up all the produce, and then I put it in large glass jars or containers ready to be used. If you've ever watched cooking shows, you'll have noticed the TV chefs make cooking look easy because all the prep is done beforehand. The same rule will apply at home—prep the ingredients ahead of time so your meals can be made in a jiffy!

REDUCTIONISM

In *A Zero Waste Life*, I discuss the concept of reductionism, which is an approach to lowering your meat consumption. If you are already a vegan or vegetarian, that's great! But having a chosen dietary restriction is a privileged lifestyle choice, and adopting a more flexible concept like reductionism might be more sustainable for most people and families. Meat production is one of the greatest contributors to greenhouse gas emissions, and of course there are ethical and moral considerations tied to our industrial meat production. Here are some ways you could consider reducing your meat consumption.

1. MEAT-FREE (MON)DAYS – Choose a day of the week where the whole family eats vegan or vegetarian meals. This is a great way to try some new recipes and ease into meat-free meals. If you are unsure how your family will react, you could just quietly start making meatless recipes using ingredients and flavors everyone likes once a week. Chances are most people won't even notice.

2. QUALITY OVER QUANTITY – If you do eat meat, aim to buy the best quality meat you can afford. Consider buying meat that is sourced locally and reared by farmers who care about the welfare of their animals. It will be more expensive, but that's not necessarily a total negative: the price will mean that you will eat less of it, so the overall impact on your budget will be minimal. Because it is more valuable, and also because it tastes better, I guarantee that you will not want to waste any of this higher quality meat. Another idea is to only eat meat on special occasions, like I did as a young child. This might mean only eating meat when you're going out to dinner, or when you are hosting a dinner party or an extended family get-together.

3. CHANGE YOUR THINKING – Instead of thinking that eating less meat is about depriving yourself, try to flip your mindset and think of it as an opportunity to sample an abundance of fruits and vegetables instead. Get creative with trying new recipes and

experimenting with new types of fruits and vegetables. A fun idea is to take your children to the local Asian, Indian or Middle Eastern grocery store and walk around the aisles, choosing new (package-free) produce they would like to try. It's a great way for children to connect with different types of foods.

4. **ZERO WASTE DIET** — If none of these options seem right for you, consider that by eating a package-free diet, you are also automatically embarking on what I call the "zero waste diet." By eating package-free foods, you are inevitably choosing items that are less processed, have fewer additives and preservatives, and are much better for you and your family. This is a fantastic side-effect of living a zero waste life—simply by reducing your packing waste, you will be eating healthier!

FOOD STORAGE

Storing your produce properly is vitally important for reducing food waste. Here are some simple tips to help extend the life of your fresh foods.

- • LEAFY GREENS – Wrap in newspaper or a damp cloth so that they last longer in the refrigerator.

- • LOOSE SALAD LEAVES – Wash and dry in a salad spinner and then store in an airtight container.

- • CELERY AND HERBS – Chop the leafy ends off the celery and store the stalks in a jar of water. Herbs can also be stored in a jar of water to extend their life.

- • ROOT VEGETABLES – These should be stored somewhere dry and cool, such as in a basket underneath the sink.

- • CITRUS FRUITS – These can be stored in a bowl on the countertop, away from direct sunlight.

ZERO WASTE KITCHEN

The kitchen is the heart of the home. The easiest zero waste swaps also begin in the kitchen. As a quick exercise, look at all the gadgets, devices, tools, utensils and kitchen "essentials" that you have in your kitchen. Then rewind to when you were a child—how many of these items existed then? If you go even further back and imagine your grandparents' kitchen, did they have any of these items? Sure, some of the modern items we have are needed for convenience, but most of them aren't needed at all.

Today is the day we start examining what we really need in the kitchen to make delicious and nutritious meals without waste. We can better organize our kitchens so we can make simple meals without packaging and without waste.

By following these simple steps, you'll be able to turn your kitchen into a zero waste haven.

START WITH A CLEAN SLATE

1. **DO A KITCHEN AUDIT** – Open up all the cupboards in your kitchen and take stock of everything you have. Start going through drawers and cupboards, and do a visual assessment of all the tools, crockery, gadgets and utensils you have.

2. **DECLUTTER** – Start removing any items you haven't used for more than a year and you don't intend to use in the near future. Be realistic about this. Consider your lifestyle, and what your family likes to eat. Put everything you don't use in a box to be donated or sold. Make room for your new way of life.

3. **DO A PANTRY AUDIT** – Remove everything from your pantry. Group similar items together—this will help identify how many duplicates you have. Check use-by dates, and compost those things that can no longer be salvaged and used. If you find you have products you know you're never going to use, donate them to a local food bank, shelter or other charity that wants long-life food. Next, make a list of everything in your pantry in a notes document in your phone, so you know exactly what you have before you buy anything new, or stick the list on the door of the pantry so that everyone in the family can see what's in there.

4. **STORE EVERYTHING IN GLASS JARS** – Remove and responsibly recycle all the excess packaging, and put all the pantry items into glass jars. You can label them with a glass marker or a permanent marker on some masking tape. Using glass jars ensures you can see everything in your pantry clearly. What you can't see, you won't

use. This is also a great preparation for zero waste shopping habits you might develop in the future, because bulk stores allow you to bring your own containers and transfer everything directly to your own storage devices. Remember to use what you have first, so start stockpiling and upcycling glass jars, or raid your neighbor's recycling bin or your work recycling bin. Also check "freecycle" sites and Facebook swap groups. Wash recycled jars thoroughly and use them to store everything in your pantry. If you need larger jars, or still don't have enough, try secondhand stores. You can often get large, good quality jars for a few dollars.

5. **CLEAN OUT YOUR FRIDGE** – Now it's time to clean out your fridge. Remove all items past their use-by date and clean all the shelves. Create an "eat first" box in which to place all the items in the fridge that are close to their use-by date or on their last legs. Label the box and put it on the top shelf of your fridge so that everyone in the household knows to use these items first.

KITCHEN RULES

1. **EAT DOWN YOUR STORES** – Over the next thirty days it's time to get creative and eat down your stores. Most of us have hoarded food in the past, more food than would be necessary even for emergency situations. If you have too many cans of chickpeas, start looking up recipes to use them. If you have too many types of pasta, start using them in pasta bakes and other meals. See it as a challenge to eat down your stores and start fresh with a decluttered pantry.

2. **THE RULE OF TWOS** — Now that we have a clean slate, we can start buying ingredients for your zero waste kitchen. For pantry staples, I apply the rule of twos, which just means to only buy two items of the same category. This is a great way to make sure you don't overbuy and start hoarding food again. Only buy two types of pasta, a long type and a short type, and eat those before you buy more. Choose two legumes—for example, chickpeas and lentils— eat those and then buy more. This ensures there is enough variety and at the same time limits the amount of food accumulated in your pantry. You can apply this rule for all your pantry needs— everything from types of oils, types of rice and even types of snacks. You can extend the rule of twos for emergency situations or if you live in a rural location by having enough food for your whole family for two weeks.

FOOD SHOPPING

In *A Zero Waste Life*, I provide a complete guide on how to do your first zero waste shop. The key is to put together a zero waste shopping kit that you have handy by the front door, ready to take with you on your bulk store trips or when you go to the supermarket.

My zero waste shopping kit consists of:

- shopping bags—invest in sturdy ones with thick handles
- produce bags for loose items
- jars for items at the bulk store
- glass containers for meats, fish and dairy products.

ZERO WASTE SHOPPING

FOR PEOPLE WHO DON'T LIVE NEAR A BULK STORE

One of the questions I get asked most frequently is, "What do I do if I don't live near a bulk store?" My answer is just try your best and adopt the following zero waste shopping hacks.

1. CHOOSE METAL, GLASS OR CARDBOARD OPTIONS – Most foods can be bought in more sustainable packaging than plastic. Choose one of these better options and recycle the packaging responsibly.

2. SHOP FROM THE OUTER AISLES OF THE SUPERMARKET – This is usually where the fresh and naked produce resides. If you shop the outer aisles, there is less processed food and, therefore, less plastic packaging.

3. SHOP LESS – Most products that are sold packaged are dry goods, which have long shelf lives. If you don't have a bulk store near you, but you have one within driving distance, you could consider making the trip just once a month for all your dry goods.

4. GET IT DELIVERED – Many bulk stores and produce grocers actually offer a delivery service. If you can't make it to the store, get the products delivered, but make sure you ask about their packaging policy first.

ZERO WASTE HOME

My mother is a superwoman, there's no doubt about it. She grew up with a communist work ethic instilled in her by my grandfather, who worked every day of his life. She is my absolute hero for running a household, working six or seven days a week, raising two children, going to night school and building a life in a country where she barely knew the language. My father was a great help, of course, but my mother was the engine that powered the ship.

My mother's hardworking spirit is something she applies to her home life too. She runs the household with efficiency, cleanliness and order, all on a dime. Whenever a guest enters her home, the first thing they comment on is how clean and tidy everything is, and she beams with pride each time. She is the one who taught me the best cost-saving household tips, which also happen to be planet-saving as well. When applying zero waste principles to the home, I always think of my mother, so this chapter is dedicated to her.

ZERO WASTE HOME PRINCIPLES

1. Sweep every day.
2. Clean once a week.
3. Deep clean once a season.

There are many cleaning and home tidying guides out there, but I find the above principles, taught to me by my mother, to be simple and effective.

1. **SWEEP EVERY DAY** – In traditional Asian households, as well as many other cultures, you often see the caretaker of the house sweeping high-traffic areas daily. This means giving floors a quick sweep or vacuum, as well as wiping down countertops with an all-purpose cleaner.

2. **CLEAN ONCE A WEEK** – This means vacuuming, cleaning the bathroom and kitchen, dusting, mopping, emptying out the recycling and tending to the compost. Your children should be a part of this—you can assign them chores that are suitable for their age (and plan the chores on your household command station, as discussed in Day 6). You can employ a reward system for the chores, but I generally like to make it part of the family rules that everyone does their chores without complaint. Living in a tidy, clean home should be reward enough.

3. **DEEP CLEAN ONCE A SEASON** – At the beginning of a new season, I like to do a deep clean, which involves decluttering and cleaning out areas that are often forgotten. I suggest going through the three-day decluttering challenge outlined in *A Zero Waste Life* every three months to ensure you maintain a clutter-free home. This is also a time to clean windows, garages or hidden cupboards, and it might be a good time to do a "reset" of your pantry and fridge.

MINIMALIST AND ZERO WASTE CLEANING RECIPES

You'll notice most of the recipes in this book use five or fewer ingredients, almost all of which can be found in your pantry. I deliberately made the recipes as simple as possible, because I want it to be *easier* to make your own cleaning products than it is to go to a supermarket and buy the product off the shelf.

ALL-PURPOSE CLEANER

1 part castile soap : 10 parts water – Mix together in an upcycled spray bottle and wipe with some homemade cleaning cloths.

Castile soap is an olive-oil-based soap that can be used for many purposes. I buy this in liquid form from the bulk store, but you can also make your own. Buy a castile soap bar and grate it using a cheese grater, then add the grated soap to a large pot with two liters of hot water. Stir until the grated soap has dissolved and let it cool, then decant into a two-liter container for storage.

Homemade cleaning cloths are a great way to recycle old cotton T-shirts, linens, towels or other unwanted textiles. Cut the material to whatever size you need and store the cloths in a basket for easy access. When you use one, you can just pop it in the wash and use it again. If you have old textiles that are too worn out or are not suitable for use as cloths (such as lace), you can take them to any H&M clothing store, which accepts all textiles for recycling, or search the web for "textile recycling near me" to find somewhere that will accept your used textiles.

GLASS CLEANER

1 part white vinegar : 4 parts water – Mix together in an upcycled spray bottle and wipe clean with newspaper. It leaves a streak-free finish and is also a great way to reuse newspaper, or any type of thin tissue paper you may have around the home.

APPLIANCE CLEANER

2 parts white vinegar : 2 parts lemon juice : 1 part water – Mix together in an upcycled spray bottle and spray onto surfaces with grease or food stains. Leave for about ten minutes and then scrub away with a coconut scourer or a bamboo scrubbing brush.

REMOVING LABELS
FROM GLASS CONTAINERS

When starting on your zero waste journey, you don't need to go out and buy new glass containers. The best zero waste option is to use what you already have. Pump bottles and glass jars are my absolute favorites for refilling items. I remove all traces of the old labels to make them more aesthetically pleasing.

To remove sticky labels, just blast the label with a hairdryer to loosen the glue and remove as much of the label as you can. For any residual stickiness, make a paste with equal parts coconut oil and bicarbonate of soda and then scrub away!

ZERO WASTE LAUNDRY

Laundry is possibly one of the most boring topics in the world to talk about. However, I promise that once you apply this zero waste laundry method, everything will be simpler and much easier to manage!

First, we need to put together a zero waste laundry kit. Applying my "three steps to zero waste" method discussed in Day 2, it's always best to *reduce* your waste first, and this means using up what you already have. Once you have done so, consider assembling these zero waste laundry essentials.

1. **GUPPYFRIEND BAG OR CORA BALL** – One of the least obvious but most invasive forms of plastic pollution is microfibers shed by synthetic clothing. Polyester is one of the most common fabrics used in fashion, and it sheds microplastics when washed. This ends up in our waterways and gets eaten by sea life. It then makes its way up the food chain through a process called bioaccumulation and eventually enters human bodies. It would be wonderful if we could all avoid buying synthetic fibers, but where that's not possible, use a Cora Ball or Guppyfriend bag to filter out these microplastics during washing and prevent them from entering our waterways. The Cora Ball is a ball that you put straight into your washing machine to capture synthetic microfibers from your clothing. The Guppyfriend bag works much like a delicates bag, allowing you to put your laundry inside and capture the synthetic fibers that way. Both of them are handy and effective, so just do some research on which one might suit your lifestyle better.

2. **LAUNDRY POWDER** – A lower waste option is to choose laundry powder that comes in cardboard or paper packaging. Just make sure the brand you buy doesn't come with a plastic spoon inside and gives instructions for measuring the correct amount instead. For a zero waste option, stock up on laundry powder at your local bulk store. Bring your own container and fill with the product of your choice. Most bulk stores have liquid or powdered laundry detergent available. Another zero waste option is to make your own laundry powder.

ZERO WASTE
LAUNDRY POWDER

This is one of my favorite zero waste laundry powder recipes.
It will make enough for six washes (or more), but you can double
or triple the recipe to make more.

- 1 cup bicarbonate of soda
- 1 cup grated castile soap
- ½ cup washing soda
- ½ cup borax powder

Mix thoroughly to combine the ingredients, and store in an airtight
container. Add ½ cup to your washing machine for a load of washing.

3. **STAIN REMOVER** – I make my own stain remover from 1 part castile soap : 5 parts water and store it in an upcycled spray bottle, then spray it directly onto stains before washing. Another great option is to use a stain remover soap bar, which you can buy from the supermarket. They're useful for stubborn stains and are often wrapped in paper or cardboard.

I put all my laundry essentials in a secondhand straw basket so I can easily carry them to the laundry room. Here are some other simple recipes for the rest of your laundry needs.

- **WHITE VINEGAR** – Instead of store-bought fabric softener, just add one cup of white vinegar to your laundry load. This will have the same effect of softening the fibers of your fabrics. It is also good for any smelly clothes, like workout gear or clothes that have become damp—one cup in the wash should neutralize all smells.

- **HOMEMADE WHITENER** – For a lower waste option, mix together 1 cup of hydrogen peroxide, 3 tablespoons of lemon juice and 15 cups of water. (Hydrogen peroxide will often be sold in a plastic container, but you can buy in bulk quantities to reduce packaging waste.) Store in an upcycled plastic container, and use ½ cup for each load of whites. However, more often than not, I find the zero waste option of a cup of lemon juice added to the wash and some strong sunlight to be an effective bleach for my whites.

- **STUBBORN STAIN REMOVER** – Make a paste of bicarbonate of soda and water, and rub it directly onto the stain. Let it sit for 15–20 minutes, and then wash normally.

MAKE YOUR OWN
SOAP HOLDER

Here is a great way to reuse old jar lids and any rubber bands in your home. Just hook some rubber bands over a jar lid in a grid-like pattern and you've got yourself a handy soap holder! This works so well because it allows the bar to drain and air-dry properly. You can add as many elastic bands as you want, depending on the size of your soap bar. This is a great DIY hack for when you travel as well.

ZERO WASTE CLOTHING

My love of fashion started when I was young. Shopping served as a balm for the highs and lows of my life. If I got a job promotion, I would buy some Gucci shoes to celebrate. If I was feeling annoyed by a colleague, I would buy a new Fendi handbag to placate my anger. If I was feeling sad about a breakup, I would buy a pair of Dolce & Gabbana sunglasses to bury my pain. I equated shopping with happiness. The small dopamine hit it provided was so addictive. I justified my purchases as retail therapy—"Cheaper than actually going to therapy," I would say.

My relationship with clothing has changed since I began my zero waste and minimalism journey. My mother worked in the Australian fashion industry for over thirty years, and I saw the extensive labor that goes into the creation of each garment. Sustainable fashion companies, such as the ones my mother worked for, provide their garment workers with fair wages and good working conditions. Fast fashion, on the other hand, is tainted by blood, sweat and tears. I can no longer ignore how a $20 dress was made and who it was made by. It's made by someone like my mother, but in poor working conditions and for insufficient pay. The cheaper the garment, the poorer the working conditions. Our Earth's resources cannot sustain the influx of cheap garments into stores every week for something so trivial as fleeting fashion trends. Don't get me wrong: I love good style, but that's different from fashions, which come and go. Today is the day to embrace a new way of thinking about clothing for you and your family. Don't spend your income on disposable items. It's time to understand the true cost of the garment you're wearing.

THE ORIGIN STORY

As with the true cost of food, you can engage your children in a discussion about the clothes they are wearing. Try to spark their interest by asking questions such as:

- What do you think this garment is made of?
- Where do you think it was made?
- Who do you think made it?
- What do you think their working conditions were like?
- How much do you think they were paid? Is it sufficient for a healthy life?
- What other resources were used in the making of this garment?
- What is the true cost of the garment in terms of human labor and environmental costs?

When you start tackling these difficult questions, you and your children will soon realize that there's so much more to the history of a garment than the $20 you paid for it. This is a great way to open your children's eyes to the fact that all the "stuff" they have has been designed, made and sold by a real person, and that the planet's resources have paid for it as well.

THE LOW BUY YEAR

Stopping your shopping is the easiest way to start embracing a "less, but better" philosophy for all your clothing purchases. In 2020, I embarked on an ambitious project called the Low Buy Year. There are many versions of the Low Buy Year challenge; however, my focus was to only buy twenty items in 2020. Here are the rules for the Low Buy Year:

1. I am allowed to replace things that I've used up.

2. I am allowed to buy five items per season (twenty items for the whole year). Only secondhand items can be purchased.

3. I will create a realistic budget for myself and stick to it.

4. I am allowed to spend money on experiences as long as I stick to my budget each week. I call this my pocket money. This is money set aside for going to dinner, buying coffee or doing things with family and friends that do not involve acquiring more stuff.

The Low Buy Year has made me reflect on why I was purchasing clothing in the first place. More often than not, it was to fill an emotional void. The process taught me to stop before I shop. I now pause to think about each purchase for a few days, asking myself the following questions:

1. Is it well made and designed to last?

2. Will it suit my lifestyle, and will I wear it again and again?

3. Does it complement my existing wardrobe?

I used to be an impulsive shopper, but this process has made me more discerning. More importantly, it has opened up the real reasons why I was shopping in the first place.

ZERO WASTE CLOTHING KIT

I was once the type of person who would find a small hole in a garment and decide it was time to buy something new. In reality, I was just looking for an excuse to spend money, and to justify my search for the dopamine hit that comes from shopping. Shopping nurtures the "gatherer" tendency in all of us. It is a seductive habit that satisfies our most basic instincts. But today is the day to change your mindset when it comes to buying something new, and learn to repair before you repurchase.

In order to help you do this, I've outlined the essentials you will need to create a zero waste clothing kit for maintaining your clothing and keeping it looking its best.

1. SEWING KIT – Put together a basic sewing kit with:
   - fabric scissors
   - thread scissors
   - stitch unpicker
   - needle and thread
   - fabric pins.

This should suffice for most of your repair needs. Skills such as sewing on a button, hemming a skirt or pants, or darning a hole might be something you can learn from friends or family, or try YouTube.

2. **STEAMER** – I've found that very few clothes actually require dry cleaning. A good steamer can make an outfit look fresher. I've even got rid of my iron, opting to steam my clothes instead. Most garments can be washed inside-out in a delicates bag on a gentle cycle. Then just air dry, and steam when the garment is dry. Another option is to gently handwash the stained area only and let it air dry.

3. **LINT ROLLER** – Keep items looking spick and span with a reusable lint roller. Most dark-colored clothing items can be made to look new again by removing built-up dust, hair and other fibers.

4. **FABRIC SHAVER** – This is a must-have implement for all your knitwear. It removes pilling that develops on wool and cashmere garments. A quick shave every season will make the garment look brand-new again.

RESPONSIBLE DISPOSAL
OF CLOTHING

In many zero waste guides and books there is a lot of emphasis on the accumulation of "zero waste" lifestyle items, but very little discussion about what happens when something needs to be discarded. The easy solution for most people is to donate the clothing item to their local charity shop, which is a great option if your garments are in good condition and still have a second life in them. My approach to zero waste living includes what sustainability architect William McDonough calls the "cradle to cradle" philosophy, which means that we must consider the life cycle of a product beyond "cradle to the grave," and seek to keep reusing the same resources as much as possible rather than using virgin materials. If we can recirculate the material back into a productive purpose, that's always the best option.

Here are some ideas for how you can consider the "cradle to cradle" approach for clothing.

1. Make reusable cleaning cloths from your old, worn-out clothing, as discussed in Day 11.

2. Donate to "dress for success" charities, homeless shelters, women's refuges or refugee resource centers.

3. Donate clothing to be used for dress-ups at schools and childcare centers.

4. Recycle your textiles at H&M retail stores or other industrial recycling collection sites.

5. Avoid sending clothing to a landfill at all costs!

HOME COMFORTS

A house is simply the four walls in which a family resides. The thing that turns a house into a home is the atmosphere we create as a family—one filled with love, tenderness and care. There is a beautiful Japanese concept called wabi-sabi, which roughly translates to something like "perfectly imperfect." It is easy to feel pressure to host the perfect family dinner or a Pinterest-worthy gathering, and often the burden of making it perfect can become so overwhelming that we might choose not to do it at all. This pressure is self-imposed, and can lead to us holding ourselves back. In my own journey toward living a truly zero waste life, I've embraced wabi-sabi. There is perfection in the imperfection.

Some of my fondest memories are of meals around the dinner table, or the annual Christmas and birthday traditions. The ideas explored in this chapter have helped fill my life with more thoughtful and meaningful rituals. Embracing the perfection in the imperfection has given me the freedom to create precious moments for my family that will linger in their memories long after I am gone, without the pressure of needing it to look perfect. It has helped me reexamine what is essential to me: good food, laughter and being present.

MAKING TIME
TO BE TOGETHER

The most difficult part of hosting a gathering or creating a family ritual is getting everyone together in the same place at the same time. Have you noticed that you often place others ahead of your own family when scheduling activities? Other people's birthday parties, weddings, even extracurricular activities are added to the calendar with great prominence, yet the simple act of eating dinner together is often sacrificed to make way for "more important" things.

Eating dinner together is one of the simplest but most significant family rituals. It places value on the meal, and gives the family time to process the day as a collective. One idea I love is to ask about the highs and lows of each day. Asking your children to name one high and one low from their day allows them to open up to you and also gives you insight into the parts of their lives you don't see. If you can, make time to eat one meal a day together—this could be breakfast or dinner. Schedule it in if you need to so you can all enjoy the ritual of sharing a meal.

ECO-CONVENIENCE MEALS

Cooking and sitting down to eat together can often feel like a mammoth task at the end of a busy day. It's easy to succumb to takeaway food, store-bought ready meals or packaged frozen meals. Many zero waste lifestyle bloggers preach against convenience foods, but the inconvenient truth is that, as parents, we need convenience. I want to introduce to you a new kind of eco-convenience meal: one that is package-free but doesn't compromise on taste, ease or convenience. This makes the task of enjoying a home-cooked meal a lot easier.

1. **INVEST IN 10–12 FREEZER-SAFE GLASS CONTAINERS** – These containers are an investment for your eco-convenience meals and can be sized to give you the right portions for single, double and family-sized meals. A good tip is to buy them all from the same brand so that they stack and fit together well for easy storage.

2. **COOK EXTRA** – When you are cooking, add extra ingredients, enough for one or two additional portions, or cook double for a whole extra meal, and then freeze the excess in your glass containers. Then, next time you are too tired to cook, all you have to do is take the container out of the freezer and reheat. This is just as convenient as any freezer meal you might buy in the supermarket, but it's more nutritious and delicious, and comes without the single-use packaging. Cooking in larger batches will also save you time and money in the long run.

3. BATCH COOKING – Spend one day a month batch cooking multiple meals that you can freeze. This can be a fun activity in which everyone gets involved. Just make sure to add extra ingredients to your shopping list for that week and have a cook up with the whole family!

4. DISCOUNTED FOODS – One thing I do to help reduce food waste is go to the supermarket at the end of the day and buy price-reduced foods. Many of the good quality prepared salads and premade meals are discounted at the end of the day. Some of them might be heavily reduced if they are close to their best-before dates. It's worth noting that "best-before" dates are different than "use-by" dates. Use-by dates are specifically for foods that may pose a health or safety risk if consumed after that date, while best-before dates are used for foods that may lose a little bit of taste or quality if consumed after that date but still remain perfectly safe to eat. Producers will often err on the side of caution when applying best-before dates, so if you consume food close to this date you might not notice any difference to the product at all. When the food has been stored correctly, there should be no cause for alarm eating foods that are past their best-before dates. Some discounted foods are also suitable to be bought and frozen to be reheated later.

CREATE A TECH BED

As soon as my husband and I come home in the evening, we put our phones and devices in the "tech bed." This is a place for our gadgets to rest while we rest. Most people's bad tech habits stem from addiction to our phones. I've found myself guilty of this, twitching for the phone, responding to every notification. It's time to break the twitch and allow yourself freedom from the matrix when you get home. Encourage everyone in the family to put their gadgets in the tech bed so you can all have a break. If children want to play games or watch shows or surf the internet, allocate half an hour a day when they can do so, not including any time spent online for school purposes, and then return the gadgets back to the tech bed.

LESS TECH, MORE LIFE

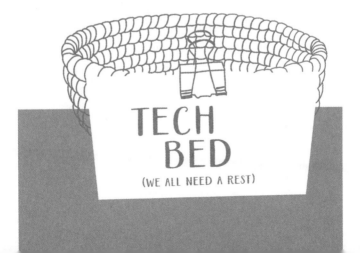

TECH BED
(WE ALL NEED A REST)

BE PRESENT

The reason many of us have our phone cameras out during family gatherings is to record our memories to save them for later and share them with others. We are preserving these precious moments for a future that might not ever come. Instead of capturing our memories for our future selves, why not be present in them instead? Take away all the distractions. You don't need a photo for every moment of the day, you need to live it. Be more mindful in the way you talk to your children—give them your undivided attention and spend time with them without being distracted by a screen. These small changes in habit will be reflected in the way your children respond to you. All they want is our time and attention—let's give it to them.

My husband and I have a "power down" hour with my daughter before she goes to bed. This means no screens (no phones, television or gadgets), and we spend the hour focused entirely on her. We dance, listen to music and talk and play with her, giving her our undivided attention. I've seen her behavior change as a result of this. She throws fewer tantrums and is calmer before bedtime.

HYGGE IN
THE HOME

Living minimally does not mean you have to forsake comfort and joy. In fact, one of my favorite concepts is "hygge"— a Danish term meaning coziness and contentment through enjoying the simple things in the home. Here are some ways you can introduce hygge into your home by providing comfort for each of your senses.

- SIGHT — Light candles to enjoy while you eat your meals, or cut some flowers from your garden and arrange them in upcycled jars.

- SMELL — Make your own home spray by selecting one or more essential oils and adding twenty to thirty drops to a spray bottle containing 1 part vodka and 3 parts water. Spray this around your home as a deodorizer. My favorite combination is ylang-ylang, bergamot and lavender.

- TOUCH — Cover soft furnishings with a cozy blanket (this is also a great way to hide any stains) and lay out a tablecloth for special occasions. Use cloth napkins for every meal.

- **TASTE** – Indulge in some tea and treats time. At regular intervals during the day, brew a big pot of tea or coffee with cups for the whole family and some plates of small bites. For younger children, you can put out a big pitcher of water flavored with diced fruit (or add some of the rhubarb mocktail mix from Day 15). This encourages people to sit down and enjoy conversation during the busy day.

- **SOUND** – Try turning off the television and enjoying some silence. I also like listening to jazz or classical music radio as a gentle soundtrack to the day.

FUN AT HOME

In 2020, many people were asked to stay indoors, which was a reminder to the world how important our homes are. The home should be an area for rest and relaxation, but it also needs to be a place for entertainment and creativity. Staying at home shouldn't be a punishment or something that induces boredom, it should be a place where everyone can have some fun. "Creativity within confines" is a term I use to inspire people to be creative within the boundaries of zero waste living, and this principle can also be applied to areas of the home. It's about being creative with a limited budget. It's about consuming less, but creating more.

These are budget-friendly family activity ideas to inspire you to do more in your home, without having to buy more stuff.

1. **FRIDAY NIGHT DISCO** – Create a playlist with your family's favorite dance hits, string up some decorations, like a mirror ball and some rotating colored lights, which can be sourced second-hand, and create a Friday night disco! Turn off the lights and dance the night away. Your children will love it, and it's also a great sleepover activity.

2. **GO GREEN** – Start a seedling garden with your children using egg cartons, plastic fruit and vegetable punnets, and some seeds. There are some helpful video tutorials online that can teach you how to grow new plants from parts of fruits and vegetables you would normally compost. A fun way to start a small garden is to grow some microgreens, which are young vegetable greens that are quick to grow and are packed full of nutrients. Some examples include radish greens, kale and baby spinach. The upcycled plastic punnets act as mini-greenhouses, and you can harvest edible microgreens in just one to three weeks, depending on which variety you choose.

3. **ART ATTACK** – Have arts and crafts days using the dry waste from your recycling bin. Magazines and newspapers make great collage and decoupage material with which to cover cardboard boxes or plastic containers. Get some craft glue and ask your children to redecorate old containers to organize things in their rooms or other areas of the house.

4. **COOK TOGETHER** – Cooking with your children helps them learn where their food comes from and, most importantly, it helps them be productive, creative and useful in the kitchen. Also, they will love the results at the end! This is also a good option for parents

who want to cook a labor-intensive recipe and need the assistance of some sous-chefs.

5. **DRESS UPS** – Have themed dress-up parties using items from your wardrobe, or outfits designed from cut-out newspaper. Some theme ideas are superheroes, villains, witches and warlocks, 1960s hippies, robots, or wherever your imagination takes you.

6. **TALENT QUEST** – One of my favorite childhood activities was the talent shows my dad held. He would make up competitions like singing, dancing or gymnastics, and my brother and I would compete against each other for the grand prize. The prize was usually something simple like who would get to choose the movie for the next movie night, or choosing a destination to visit on the weekend. Why not hold your own talent quest—get the kids involved and make it as formal or as informal as you like!

7. **PUPPET SHOWS** – My daughter loves puppet shows. Spend an afternoon decorating old socks or other clothing to transform them into a whole range of characters. This is a great craft activity for a rainy day.

8. **THEMED MOVIE EVENINGS** – These nights can be fun and thought-provoking for the whole family. You can set the theme around an environmental movie or film and discuss the topics afterward. For older children, documentaries are excellent ways to start conversations about issues affecting our planet. For younger children, it can be more subtle. You could have a *Frozen* theme night and bring up subjects such as melting ice caps and rising sea levels, or a *Jungle Book* theme and bring up problems like

endangered animals and deforestation. It doesn't have to be heavy and too serious, just a fun gateway into discussions about issues that are important to you and your family.

9. **SING-ALONG OR MUSIC NIGHT** – Get out your instruments or find some sing-along soundtracks and enjoy singing together as a family. Choose a musical, or get the kids to write their own. Another fun option is to watch one of your kids' favorite music videos and learn all the lyrics and dance moves together as a family.

10. **CREATE RATHER THAN CONSUME** – Older children especially might enjoy making homemade beauty or cleaning products. There are so many easy DIY recipes that don't require much skill. This is a chance to teach kids about their ability to create rather than just consume.

The home should be a place for everyone to relax, and an environment where people feel like they can be themselves. Less plastic means more fantastic. It means less waste, but more life.

MOCKTAIL HOUR

As parents, we might not be able to head out on the weekend to enjoy cocktail hour at a trendy bar, but we can bring some of that joie de vivre into our homes. Here is a recipe for a delicious rhubarb mocktail that everyone can enjoy.

To make the rhubarb syrup, you need:

- 6 cups of rhubarb, chopped into small pieces
- 1 cup of brown sugar
- 1 cup of water
- a pinch of nutmeg.

Put the ingredients in a slow cooker for 4–6 hours. If you don't have a slow cooker, just cook it in a pot over low heat for 1 hour, stirring occasionally. The key is to cook it nice and slowly so the sugar does not burn. Mix it thoroughly for a smoother texture and pour into a jar. This mixture will last for two weeks in the fridge.

To make the mocktail, add one teaspoon of rhubarb syrup to some carbonated water. I use a sparkling water machine called a SodaStream with reusable glass bottles to reduce my plastic waste. If you wish, you can also add a dash of gin to make the mocktail into a cocktail for the adults. This basic recipe will work for a number of different fruits and vegetables—you can experiment and discover a variety of mocktail syrups.

CHILD CARE

DAYS

16 – 30

NATURE IS NURTURE

My father always knew how to live life. The same adventuring spirit that gave him the courage to move from China to Australia with only $200 in his back pocket also translated to our childhood adventures. He created a wonderful game in which he would open the street directory and pick a green spot on the map that we'd never visited before—always a large park or reserve of some sort. His English skills were basic, but he was a master at finding a new place to explore. We would pack our rollerblades and bikes and take a drive to this new park, and enjoy a fun, low-cost day out as a family. This hunt for new green spots is where my love of nature began.

Today is the day to think about your relationship with nature. Did you have earth-loving, hippie parents who instilled in you a deep appreciation of the natural world, or do you feel only a faint connection to the land you are on? How do you feel about the air you breathe, the water you drink and the soil that grows your food? I am sure that, like most people, you take it for granted at least some of the time. For most of us, it's always been *available*. There's never been any doubt that you will be able to take a breath of fresh air or easily access clean water and food for sale at the supermarket. What if all this was taken away from you? What would you do then?

THREE MINUTES,
THREE WEEKS, THREE MONTHS

In most developed countries, there is a frenzied focus on the food that we eat. There are reality cooking shows, celebrity chefs and fad diets, and talking about your dietary restrictions has become the norm. Most people wouldn't blink an eye if you told them you're on a gluten-free, vegan or keto diet, or even all three of those diets at once! I'd like to strip back some of that frenzy and think about the rule of threes This is a shorthand way of saying that a human being will die after three minutes without breathing, three days without drinking, and three weeks without eating. We live in such privileged societies that fresh air and water are taken for granted, and we tend to focus only on the food restrictions we place upon ourselves.

Today, teach your children about the essentials of life that we take for granted. It shouldn't take an environmental crisis like a forest fire earthquake or tsunami for us to value the most fundamental elements of life: fresh air, water and food.

Taking your children out into nature and explaining to them the delicate balance of life is something we should all do as caregivers. We are not only caregivers to our children but also to the planet. We need to be environmental stewards, not for altruistic purposes, political persuasions or moral goodness, but for survival reasons. Earth is the only home we've got. There is no planet B.

Here are ten ways you can begin to get your children outdoors and experiencing the wonders of nature.

1. BACKYARD CAMPING – If camping in the wilderness is foreign to you, try backyard camping first. Borrow some equipment from friends or get it secondhand, and take the kids camping in the backyard. If you live in an apartment, ask to borrow a friend's or family member's backyard, or if you're feeling more adventurous, check out your local national park. This is a fun and low-cost way for children to understand what it means to sleep in nature. After this experience, they will be less likely to take for granted the privileges they have at home, and it will also open their eyes to the beauty of their natural surroundings.

2. VISIT YOUR LOCAL BOTANICAL GARDENS OR CONSERVATORY – City folks are often out of touch with nature and can find it hard to kindle a joy for hiking or the great outdoors. An easy transition is to start with a visit to the botanical gardens. Make an activity out of it by asking the children to choose three plants or flowers that they've never seen before and then draw them, photograph them or write a few sentences about them. Treat every excursion as an opportunity for learning. As parents, we shouldn't be afraid of being teachers too! You know your children best, so you can create activities suitable for their age and interests.

3. DISCOVER YELLOW AND BLUE SPOTS – Before the age of the internet, our street directory was the source of many surprises. My dad's handy green spot trick could also be applied to bay walks and

beaches. We couldn't google "best bay walks" in the early 1990s, so we just followed the map to find yellow spots and blue spots. We felt like pioneers, taking in Australia one colored spot at a time. We also found the best hidden gems in Sydney. We rarely went to where all the tourists hung out—it was always secret coves and hidden bays with hardly anyone in sight. I always wondered what white Australians would have thought if they had stumbled upon us, a Chinese family enjoying some fried rice on a secret beach by the Sydney seaside!

4. **VISIT ROCK POOLS** — I went to the beach often as a child, but until visiting the rock pools on a Geography class's excursion, I had never noticed the life teeming all around me. I remember my eyes being opened to the wealth and variety of living organisms that were on display once we stopped, paused and truly looked. Go to the rock pools and create a special activity associated with being there. Buy your children a sketchbook and ask them to draw what they find, then go home and ask them to identify all the creatures they sketched. You can set more creative tasks for older children: painting, writing poetry or even putting together a playlist that reminds of them of the feelings evoked.

5. **GO SWIMMING OUTDOORS** — Swimming is a way of life for many people. A lot of us swim before we can even walk. You might have a swimming pool at home, or love visiting your local public pool, but don't forget natural swimming spots like ocean pools, lakes, rivers and creeks. Swimming outdoors introduces you to tidal patterns, the differences between salt water and fresh water, and different climates and temperatures. Younger children can learn

the differences between fresh water and sea water, and how aquatic life differs from place to place. Older children can begin to develop an understanding of how climate and weather are different; they can interpret short-term weather patterns, but see the effects of climate change.

6. **TAKE A TRAIN TO A RURAL OR REGIONAL TOWN** – On the weekend, pick a rural or regional town on the train line, pack some lunch and go on an adventure! I've seen some of the finest fruit farms, vineyards, and beautiful, scenic country towns, and it's given me a deep appreciation for the land. Seeing where your food comes from and how it is grown and sourced is incredibly humbling. This is another way to open your children's eyes to a life that is different than theirs.

7. **TAKE THEM TO A FARMERS' MARKET** – My favorite Sunday activity with my daughter is to go to our local farmers' market. When I lived in San Francisco's Bay Area, we would go every Sunday to get fresh peaches, grapes and other seasonal fruits. All the vendors knew us as "the Australians" and would greet us with a sample of their goods. My daughter loved the sights and smells of the market, and particularly loved the cut-up fruit they handed to her as samples. Exploring a farmers' market will demonstrate to children that food doesn't just come from a plastic package in the supermarket. Ideally, interacting with the people who produce their food will help children appreciate the process and hard work that goes into getting their dinner to the table. Food brings families together; parents should nurture a love of food from an early age.

8. **TEACH THEM A NEW OUTDOOR SPORT** – Children love to learn! They also need to be occupied, and learning a new sport is a great way to exert their boundless energy. In the early 1990s, my brother and I both enjoyed rollerblading. As we grew older, we embarked on downhill mountain biking. Sport is a great way to get outdoors and socialize, and it doesn't have to be formal or organized. When was the last time you enjoyed sport without it being an "extracurricular activity"? Embrace the spontaneous joy of kicking a ball or riding a bike, without it being an organized game or with the goal of losing weight. By enjoying sport for the sake of it you will model this behavior for your kids, which will serve them well in the long run.

9. **WALK EVERYWHERE** – A great way to get outside and make running errands more interesting for your kids is to ditch the car and walk. Plan out a route—to the local shops, the library or a park—and walk it. Avoid walking during the hottest part of the day, especially in summer. Getting around without the car is an excellent way to see new sights and explore your community.

10. **FORAGE FOR YOUR FOOD** – Many of us walk around our parks and forests without taking any notice of the abundance of food around us. Why not try foraging for some edible foods and flowers? For young children, look around your neighborhood for fruit trees, herbs and vegetables in community gardens or neighborhood growing plots. If your children are older, you could borrow a book from the library about locally grown edible plants to take with you on your next family foraging outing. Just make sure you supervise your children and check what they have foraged before they take a bite out of anything.

FREEDOM WITHIN BOUNDARIES

Have you noticed that whenever children have an overwhelming number of options, they actually do less with their time? A deluge of choices causes our brains to freeze. Even as adults, we feel a slight anxiousness associated with a blank page or schedule: the options overwhelm us, and we often end up doing nothing at all. That's why living a zero waste life has actually allowed me more freedom. Living within the confines of zero waste has eliminated a lot of the excess decision-making about trivial things. It has also challenged me to find solutions to living a full life within these boundaries. Zero waste living has made me more creative and given me more freedom, more life.

Here are some ways we can enforce boundaries for our children, to help them focus on the things that matter most.

TOYS

If you're like me, you will know the feeling when the house has been overtaken by toys and they seem to be breeding overnight. To reduce clutter, we have to reduce the number of toys in the household. It's important not to view this as being cruel by restricting the number of toys your kids have: you're actually giving them the freedom to fully enjoy what they have. When children are overwhelmed by choices, they will not be satisfied with any of their toys and may engage with them *superficially*, playing with one toy for a few seconds and then dropping it to play with another. This scattered playtime habit can prevent them from being creative and shorten their attention span. Reducing the number of their toys will allow them to play *deeply*, getting creative with what they have and appreciating their toys more.

Here is a step-by-step process for how to prevent clutter and allow your children to enjoy their toys more.

1. Begin by choosing suitable storage boxes from the options you already have in your home. This could be a wooden toy chest, a large basket or even a cardboard box that your children can decorate with paint or decoupage. This is the "boundary" for their toys, and all the toys should be able to fit into these containers; if they overflow, it's time to declutter. I like to apply the "rule of twos" for toy baskets and have two baskets for each child.

2. Declutter the toys. As discussed in Day 7, it's important to get your children involved in this process. Ask them to choose their favorite toys and put them in the chosen containers. Explain to

them that the toys that do not fit will be donated to children who have less than they do, to help them understand the idea of sharing resources and giving to those in need.

3. Maintain this new standard. Adopt the "one in, one out" rule, meaning that if your child wishes to bring something new into the home, something has to leave. This also applies to any toys that are gifted to them. This habit will encourage children to be more discerning about the stuff they bring into the home and also foster a habit of being mindful about their waste.

THE TREASURE BOX

As a parent, it is easy to be sentimental and want to keep everything our children have ever made. It's also hard for children to part with keepsakes, mementos and other treasures they've accumulated over the years. Today is the day to pare back the number of sentimental items to those that are most meaningful by creating a treasure box for your children. Take your children to an antiques or secondhand store and ask them to pick out a special box for their treasures. I have a beautiful wooden box I found on the side of the road—it is hand carved and decoupaged, and will be repurposed as my daughter's treasure box when she is older. In addition to the treasure box, I like to keep a special folder that holds certificates and artwork. These two items are the "boundaries," and within these boundaries your children can choose to keep whatever they want.

Ask your children to store all their favorite things in their treasure box and folder, and help them responsibly discard everything else. It is good to do this activity together so you can aid your children, but older children many want to go through their items privately. Spread out all their sentimental items on the floor and go through them one by one. Do they really need every Christmas card they've ever received? Do they need to keep every artwork they have done since kindergarten?

More often than not, you'll find it harder to get rid of items than your children will, but let them guide you on this. You might be putting your own emotional baggage on items they place no value in. Remember, this is an exercise for them, not you. If needed, you can also create your own treasure box and folder for keepsakes and sentimental items that remind you of special times with your children, but remember to practice what you preach and not let these overflow.

This exercise will give more freedom to your special personal belongings. Storing them in a box rather than hiding them away in a drawer or on some dusty shelf allows you to easily and frequently peruse the items at your leisure. The same applies to artworks and certificates of achievement: putting them in one folder allows you easy access to them for you to enjoy looking at them again and again.

HOBBIES

The amount of stuff one can accumulate to be creative or to engage in a hobby is astounding! How many times have you or your children started a hobby, gone out and purchased all the shiny new things, and then run out of steam and never picked up the items again? That embroidery project, that half-knitted scarf, that scrapbook with only one page completed—so many of us have grand plans to be creative and embark on new hobbies but, at the first sign of boredom, will drop that hobby and move on to the next exciting project. Today is the day to cull those hobbies. Choose one or two creative endeavors that truly light you up and stick to those. Instead of being a jack of all trades, master one craft. Invest your time and money in one or two activities instead of jumping from one project to another.

Start the same way you did with sentimental items: put all your hobby and craft supplies in a large pile on the floor. You can edit down your own hobbies at the same time as your children are evaluating theirs. Go through each item and ask frank questions about the last time those watercolors, sticker books or artists' pencils were used. Choose an appropriately sized box each for all your hobby items, such as a shoebox or another container you have around the home, and reduce your supplies to fit that one box.

TEN THOUSAND HOURS

It takes approximately ten thousand hours of practice for a person to master a craft. Explain this to your children when they see an artwork in a gallery, hear a beautiful piece of music or admire a well-designed garment. Someone has spent thousands of hours learning about the craft, practicing it and finally mastering it.

Patience and diligence aren't rewarded in our fast-paced world, which can see our children jumping from one fad to another. Instead of always indulging in the newest craze and succumbing to the quick dopamine hit, try to aim for the deeper satisfaction that will come from the art of mastery. If your children enjoy drawing, encourage them to stick to one or two mediums and continue practicing it. If they enjoy building, ask them to explore all the possibilities of one type of material and try to become really proficient.

BORROW BEFORE YOU BUY

If your children want to explore new interests, instead of rushing out and buying brand-new equipment to indulge their whims, see if you can test it out first and try before you buy. This could mean borrowing the equipment from a friend or even renting it to see if they enjoy the activity first. This is particularly important for musical instruments and sports. If your children want to try the cello instead of the trumpet, rent a cello for a month and see if they actually enjoy it. If your children want to try hockey instead of karate, borrow a hockey stick and ball and ask them to take a few trial lessons and see how they feel before you invest in the new equipment. The price of items is so cheap nowadays, we often think that buying the item doesn't cost that much, but it adds up! All those extra purchases of $20 here and $50 there cost a lot in the long run. It's also important to think about the environmental impact of all this extra stuff—the virgin materials used to create the product and the landfill it will generate when it is no longer wanted. If your children want to expand their interests, borrow before you buy.

ZERO WASTE BABY

My baby girl has opened up a whole new world to me. She has made me softer (literally and metaphorically!) and also gentler. Looking at her exploring the world makes me want to work even harder to make it a better place so that she can experience the joys of life without hardship. Having a baby has also made me much more realistic about how I apply zero waste principles to my life: it's about effort, not perfection. There are things we can do every day, and some things that might just be a bit too hard due to lack of sleep or time. And that's okay.

Here are my favorite tips for reducing your waste when you have a baby. And remember, the most important thing parents can give their babies is love. It sounds corny, I know, but a baby doesn't care about "stuff"—if they are hugged, cared for and fed well, they will thrive.

DIAPERS AND WET WIPES

Modern cloth diapers are really simple and easy to use. Here is a complete rundown of how I used a combination of reusable and compostable diapers in the first years of my daughter's life.

- **TYPES AND SIZES** – Buy newborn-sized cloth diapers to be used for the first few weeks, and then you can buy adjustable diapers that will grow with the baby. Approximately twenty diapers should suffice; this will require you to wash them every 2–3 days. If you want to wash less often, buy more diapers. You can buy them secondhand or ask for them to be gifted to you for your baby shower. I chose diapers with Velcro fastenings for quick and easy changes. There are lots of different types of reusable diapers out there. I used two different kinds:

  - **ALL-IN-ONE CLOTH DIAPERS** – As the name suggests, these are all-in-one, so the inner liner is attached to the outer covering. This makes folding laundry easier, but I found that these take longer to dry.

  - **SEPARATE LINERS AND COVERS** – These are quicker to dry, and it doesn't take much effort to pair the liner and cover at folding time.

  Don't be daunted by the overwhelming amount of information and discussion about modern cloth diapers. I suggest you buy a couple of diapers in different brands and styles to experiment with and see which you like best.

- **INSTALL A BIDET ATTACHMENT TO YOUR TOILET** – You can buy a simple bidet attachment from the hardware store for around $30 and install it yourself. This acts as a handy hose so you can easily spray off the mess from dirty diapers directly into the toilet before putting the diaper in the washing machine.

- **RINSE AND WASH** – After rinsing the diapers, put them directly into the washing machine in a hot wash using a gentle washing powder. Just follow the instructions for your particular brand of cloth diapers to ensure you retain the waterproof covering.

- **SINGLE-USE DIAPERS** – If you find the idea of cloth diapers too difficult and would prefer to use disposable diapers, consider using compostable diapers. Check out the different options near you. Remember, compostable diapers need to be properly composted in industrial facilities, so a collection service is often required. I used compostable diapers in the evening, as my daughter slept through the night and this was not a habit I wanted to break, so I had a collection service pick up the dirty diapers for just a few dollars per week.

- **WET WIPES** – My midwife recommended that water and cotton cloth are the best thing for a baby's bottom, not disposable baby wipes. I had a small, wide brimmed jar filled with water in my chest of drawers, and a pile of reusable cotton cloths. I soaked the cotton cloth in the jar of water, wrung it out and used it whenever I needed to wipe my baby's bottom. I also had a reusable silicone ziplock pouch with premoistened wet cloths for when we were out and about.

- **DEDICATED DIAPER LAUNDRY BASKET** – We had a separate basket for all the dirty diaper-related items, including soiled diapers and wet cloths. Separating this from the rest of the washing prevented any cross contamination, and it was a visual reminder that these items needed a separate hot wash.

- **DRY BAG AND WET BAG** – When out and about, we had a diaper bag for all the "dry" products such as clean diapers and cotton cloths, and the soiled items were kept in a waterproof "wet" bag. This prevented cross contamination and made it a simple system for everyone to remember.

- **DIAPER RASH CREAM** – I used a cream created by my friend Stevie called Yay for Earth, which contains beeswax, organic olive oil, organic shea butter, organic pomegranate seed oil and raw honey. The recipe is on her blog, but you can also order it from her website. The product is so nice that I've been using it for my face as well. Another good alternative is coconut oil, which helps provide a protective barrier and is super moisturizing. In France, they use a diaper cream called liniment, made of olive oil and limewater (also known as calcium hydroxide solution), that you can make yourself and store in a glass pump bottle. You can use this on reusable cotton cloths instead of baby wipes.

MAKE SECONDHAND YOUR FIRST CHOICE

I bought my stroller, crib, baby carrier, baby bath and changing mat all secondhand. The only thing I didn't buy secondhand was the car seat, because safety standards for these change regularly, and it's best to get a car seat that complies to the latest safety standards to prevent on-the-spot fines. Here are some suggestions for where you can look for preloved baby gear that still has a lot of life in it.

- ONLINE STORES – Trawl Craigslist, Facebook Marketplace or similar sites for secondhand baby clothes. The internet offers a wealth of sites from which to buy secondhand baby clothes. Look for good deals and, ideally, shop local.

- THRIFT STORES AND GARAGE SALES – Discover (or rediscover) your local charity shop. They can have amazing, and often brand-new, baby clothes and accessories. Garage sales can also be absolutely full of baby gear in great condition for next to nothing. Just give anything you buy a hot wash before your baby uses it.

- CREATE A SWAP BOX – A great way to reduce your waste is to swap items instead of buying them new. Whenever my daughter outgrows her clothes or toys, I put them in a box and label them with her age ("1–2 years," for example). I then trade this with other parents who have boxes with clothing and toys for older children.

The boxes can be refilled and continually passed around families with children of different ages.

- BUY FROM ETHICAL BRANDS – If you do want to indulge in something new, remember to go slow and buy what you need from the most ethical brands you can find. There are so many local suppliers who make their products by hand, so support these artisans. My daughter's two favorite winter cardigans were bought from an artisan fair, and because they were extremely well made from quality materials, they have stood the test of time after multiple washes.

MAKE IT YOURSELF

- **FABRIC WIPES** – Old flannel sheets or cotton clothing can be cut up into small squares to make cleaning cloths for dirty fingers, faces or bottoms. I found squares approximately 20 cm x 20 cm to be the right size.

- **ALMOND OIL, JOJOBA OR COCONUT OIL** – Despite the huge number of baby products out there, my midwife recommended that a baby only needs water to be cleaned in their first year. If they experience some skin dryness, you can use a light, absorbent oil such as almond, jojoba or coconut oil as a massage oil.

- **BABY FOOD** – Use a high-speed blender to make your own organic baby food with no plastic waste. I collected small, freezer-safe glass jars and froze the food in single portions for easy access. You can also batch cook and freeze larger portions. When we were heading out for the day, I warmed the food at home and stored it in a thermos. A long-handled teaspoon proved to be handy for getting to the bottom of the thermos.

BREASTFEEDING

- **BREAST PADS AND NURSING BRAS** – If you are breastfeeding, you can buy amazing reusable bamboo breast pads, as well as cloth nursing pads and postpartum pads. Make sure you also invest in good quality nursing bras that will withstand the test of time so you don't have to replace them as frequently.

- **FREEZE BREASTMILK** – Breastmilk can be stored in glass jars in the freezer. I used glass baby bottles from a brand called Lifefactory, which have a silicone sleeve to make them less slippery, for safety.

THE BETTER
BABY REGISTRY

A friend or family member having a baby on the way is a source of excitement and joy, and it's tempting to rush out and buy new, shiny things to celebrate the upcoming birth. However, like most parents, I've received unwanted gifts that are actually more of a hindrance than a help. Here are some suggestions of ways you can give new parents better gifts.

1. DO YOUR HOMEWORK – Ask your friends who are parents what they consider to be essentials for new babies. One of my friends suggested zip-up onesies when I was pregnant—this proved to be a revelation and really made changing our newborn so much easier!

2. ASK THE PARENTS – Ask the expectant parents what they would like. A lot of these decisions can be quite personal and, especially if it's not their first child, often they won't need a thing and may request a gift voucher or even money instead. Respect their wishes and get them something they actually need.

3. GIFT TIME INSTEAD OF STUFF – Remember that giving the gift of time or help can be so much more useful than purchased gifts. For new parents, a home-cooked meal, a few hours of help to do laundry or batch cooking, or babysitting their other children might be the best gift. Some parents might be too embarrassed or too overwhelmed to receive guests in their home, so suggest to them that you can just leave parcels of food at their door and text them when it is there, so they don't need to greet you and can collect the food at their convenience. One of my friends suggested delivering jars of homemade green smoothies so that I could have some quick and easy snacks, which was a godsend for me, and I'm sure any new parent would feel the same about any home-delivered meals.

ZERO WASTE CHILDREN

As my daughter grows up, her needs will be different, and we will have to adapt our zero waste habits accordingly. After World War I, students in many countries learned thrift education as part of their school curriculum. This involved teaching careful spending habits, and home economics classes such as cooking and sewing. It's time to bring back the thrifty mindset to our children.

ENJOY THE FREE STUFF

The most environmentally friendly solution is always to make use of what you have. It's time to get creative with your children about activities that can be enjoyed with little or no money spent. Here are some examples of craft projects that can both entertain your children and make use of things you'll already have around the home.

- **LET NATURE BE YOUR MUSE** – Collect fallen leaves, flowers or rocks, and paint them, string them into necklaces or dry them for decoration. Borrow a book from the library about nature crafts and let your imagination go wild!

- **WASTE IS NOT WASTE UNLESS WE SAY IT IS** – Why not reuse all of your dry trash and recycling for art projects? Egg cartons make great paint pots, and plastic punnets make great containers for craft supplies that can be painted and decorated as well. Shoeboxes are the ultimate craft find—they can be decoupaged with magazine cuttings and clear glue, they can be painted to form houses for toys and dolls, they can be drawn on, painted on or wrapped. Think outside the box—literally!

- **HOLIDAY PROJECTS** – Themed projects such as Christmas cards, Easter baskets and Halloween decorations are a great way to be creative using what you already have. Use newspaper, cardboard, string or whatever you have on hand to make creative decorations. Secondhand stores are also a great place to source materials.

PARTICIPATE IN THE SHARE ECONOMY

- **JOIN COMMUNITY EVENTS** – It's surprising how many people don't know what taxpayer-funded resources and activities are available in their communities. Our local library has story time, rhyme time and indigenous story time, and loads of other free activities for children that we take advantage of every week. Finding fun and free or low-cost entertainment for your children might require the use of your detective skills, but once you know what's out there, these activities are a great way to be part of the community.

- **JOIN A TOY LIBRARY** – For a small weekly subscription fee, you can access a toy library. As parents, we often think buying a toy and gifting something to our children is a true sign of love. However, children's attention spans and memory are still developing, and their attachments to material objects may be fleeting. Instead of buying them all the toys they want, which will clutter the entire home, why not join a toy library so you can borrow toys and swap them as your child grows? This is a great way to keep young minds active and prevent clutter and overconsumption at the same time.

- **MAKE YOUR OWN SWAP GROUP** – Get a small reusable storage container with a lid and fill it with toys your children no longer use. Group them and label them according to age groups. Create a swap group on Facebook or your local bulletin board with instructions on how to swap toys according to which age group you require. This is a simple way to meet new people, gain new toys and get rid of clutter!

FIX BEFORE YOU THROW AWAY

Start teaching your children that there is no such thing as "away." When we throw something in the bin, it goes to a landfill. We can teach children that the value of an item extends beyond its monetary worth, and we can start addressing the problem of landfills by fixing our things! This means learning to repair a broken toy with the power of superglue and some tape. It might also mean polishing shoes or mending a hole in a jumper. By teaching your children these basic skills, you might end up learning something yourself as well. Learning to fix their things will also give them a sense of accomplishment and instill in them a sense of creativity, ingenuity and resourcefulness, skills that are rarely taught these days when things are so cheap and easy to replace.

CHORES

Chores can be, well, a real chore! Here's a guide on how to incorporate chores into your household so that everyone plays their part.

- **COLLECTIVE AGREEMENT** – Involve the entire family to set age-appropriate chores for each person. Organize a family meeting and set some chore rules, with rewards for completing them (if you choose to do so) and consequences for not doing them. Incorporate your new zero waste habits, such as tending to the compost bin, taking out the recycling and organizing soft plastics recycling, into the chores cycle.

- **VISUAL AIDS** – As we've discussed, the chores roster should form part of your command station. It should be simple, no more than one page, and visually appealing. Print or draw pictures and put them on magnets or pushpins to help keep track of tasks, whatever suits your family and command station.

- **TEACHING CHILDREN HOW TO ADULT** – "Adulting" is another term for the basic skills of living, and these need to be taught at home. Simple things such as the ability to do laundry, cook meals, perform basic home repair and maintenance, and house cleaning—we can't let our children leave the home without having picked up these skills. If you teach your children how to do their chores properly, the knowledge will serve them well into adulthood.

- **CONSISTENCY IS KEY** – For children to successfully change their habits and learn new skills, it's important to be consistent. This means consistency in their routine (that is, the timing of the chores), and also the rewards given. Inconsistency diminishes the importance of the activity. The same principle applies to the zero waste lifestyle. You don't need to do zero waste perfectly every day, but you do need to have consistency. Effort over perfection! It also means you need to be consistent with your parenting. If you have a partner, discuss with them what your united response will be when a child doesn't do their chores, and make sure you explain the consequences to your children as well.

FUN WITHOUT SACRIFICE

- **BACKLASH** – When leading your family through lifestyle changes, you may experience some backlash. Change is difficult for children, but they can also be incredibly adaptable! When a kid doesn't want to do something, they quickly become Secret Service–grade negotiators. The key is to be honest and transparent. Discuss the realities of money with your kids. Tell them how you work to earn your money, and let them know one of the benefits of living a more eco-friendly lifestyle is that you will save some money. Explain that this thrifty way of living will allow you to spend more time together as a family without you worrying about the stresses of money. Also discuss with them the realities of our environmental impact. For young children, child-friendly shows on environmentalism can help emphasize the point. For older children, consider going on excursions to recycling plants or landfill sites, or even just take them to the back of your local shopping center where the waste disposal is. This visual indication of how wasteful our society is will encourage them to want to do better.

- **KEEPING UP WITH THE KARDASHIANS** – Children want to fit in at school and have what other children have. I remember that I never felt as if I fit in when I was growing up in the 1990s. I was often the only Chinese kid in a sea of white faces, and to me at the time, fitting in meant buying the latest fads. My poor parents paid the price, succumbing to my nagging for more Barbies, more Spice Girls postcards, thousands of stickers—and then there was the horse phase. From the ages of eight to ten, I was obsessed with horses, buying books on horse riding, sticking large posters of different stallions on the wall and even persuading my parents to get me a few equestrian lessons. My parents worked seven days a week to put food in our mouths, and here I was requesting equestrian lessons! It's okay to let your children know that different families have different priorities, and that comparing themselves to the Kardashians or any other reality TV stars is not worthwhile. Encourage them to fit in as themselves, not because of the stuff they have.

- **LEAD WITH GRACE** – Changing habits, living more mindfully and leaving a gentler footprint on the planet can be a real shock to the system for children who are used to having whatever they want. However, the good news is that children model your values. If you lead with grace, and embrace a "waste not, want not" attitude, you can make a long-lasting, positive impression on your child, no matter their age.

ZERO WASTE TEENAGERS

Whoever said one person can't change the world obviously had not heard of Greta Thunberg. A Swedish teenage environmental activist known for her straight-talking style, Thunberg started a one-person protest in August 2018 outside the Swedish parliament building, skipping school and holding up a sign reading, "school strike for the climate." Less than a year later, she had rallied millions of students and others around the world to join her strike and engage in the largest climate protests in history. This resulted in her being named *Time* magazine's Person of the Year in 2019 and being nominated for two consecutive Nobel Peace Prizes in 2019 and 2020. All this was accomplished by the time she was just seventeen years of age.

The teenage years are rife with change and rebellion. As a parent you may feel that you'll never be cool enough, smart enough or really just *enough* for your teenage child. The best way to tackle this is to give gentle guidance and provide them with positive role models, like Greta.

Eco-anxiety is a common issue that has arisen in the past few years due to the onslaught of doomsday headlines, catastrophic climate conditions and the multitude of television shows, books and movies about post-apocalyptic worlds. Eco-anxiety is a very real thing, and we shouldn't dismiss it—our children are worried about their futures and the state of the planet. However, it's time to transform that anxiety into action. It's time to be an eco-warrior, not just an eco-worrier.

Here are some practical tips on how to raise eco-warriors.

1. **AWARENESS** – In many situations, when we embark on a change, we want everyone to be as enthusiastic as we are, but in reality most people don't care. This is especially true for teenagers. The real change occurs when we can teach, rather than preach our newfound passions. This begins with awareness. Awareness about environmental issues can be encouraged in many ways. I suggest watching a documentary as a family; David Attenborough has presented some excellent programs about climate change. You could also do a bin audit. In *A Zero Waste Life*, I proposed doing a bin audit in order to fully understand what we are wasting in our homes. Put on some reusable gloves and do a bin audit with your family! Do some research on what can and can't be recycled in your area, and see what the most common items going to landfill are—it will be eye-opening.

BAADER-MEINHOF EFFECT

Also known as the frequency illusion, this is the phenomenon when something you've just learned about or discussed suddenly seems to crop up everywhere. It's a form of cognitive bias, and it will inevitably occur once you start on your zero waste journey. You'll begin to notice the plastic on our beaches, the overflowing garbage bins and the amount of single-use packaging everywhere.

Awareness is a good thing—it's the start of something bigger. Let your teenagers become more aware of the world around them and familiarize them with the issues surrounding waste, and before you know it, they'll be the ones pulling you up on your plastic packaging faux-pas.

2. **BE INFORMED, NOT INFLUENCED** – Once your children become aware of the waste issue, get them to educate themselves on what this means and how it impacts their lives. Encourage them to start following social influencers with a zero waste ethos, watch online videos explaining plastic waste, read books on the issue and ask them to fact-check everything they read and watch. It's important for them to question their social and mainstream media consumption, and not take everything at face value. We want them to ask questions, interrogate the status quo, make discerning decisions and, ultimately, make the right choices according to their values. Encourage them to be informed, not influenced. This is a key skill that should be fostered into adulthood. We live in an era of "fake news," and the wide dissemination of misinformation means that we all have to be fact-checkers in order to truly understand the issues.

3. **IMMERSION** – One of the best things I've ever done is volunteer my time. I have volunteered at a number of different organizations, including at the emergency department in a hospital, at an Aboriginal youth center and in Fiji, working with rural communities to promote health awareness. All these experiences have greatly enriched my life. They changed the course of what I wanted to do with my life and, most importantly, the type of person I wanted to become. Ask your children to begin volunteering their time to a worthwhile cause. Start small, maybe a few hours a month, and see if this can be increased. If this doesn't suit your schedule, consider volunteering for a block of time, such as in the school holidays. There are many volunteering

organizations that give teenagers the chance to experience life in remote indigenous communities, for example, or travel overseas with not-for-profit organizations. Find something that suits their interests, and be sure to do your research to ensure it is an ethical volunteer organization. The key is to be consistent. Regular volunteering helps to snap us out of our privileged mindsets. I remember when I was a bratty fifteen-year-old, my father took my family to visit the village in rural China where his family lived. Understanding more about how hard my father had worked to emigrate to Australia made me realize that being popular at school or the number of friends on my social media didn't mean a thing. Volunteering will snap teenagers out of their bubbles and open their eyes to a bigger world.

4. **CONSISTENCY** – All these steps must be followed up with consistency. The key to making sustainable changes is to switch your mindset and transform your habits. Now that your teens are armed with the knowledge that the world is bigger and there are so many important issues of which to be conscious, they can start the journey to a lifetime of positive impact, starting with themselves. The zero waste lifestyle should be driven by their own shifting mindset and a willingness to make a difference in their own lives. We often hear about the need for a top-down approach, such as policy and law reforms. This is definitely important, but to achieve these big revolutions we need to engage a new wave of activists, and this starts with individual actions. Making small changes will lead to larger cumulative difference and will create the next generation of eco-warriors.

ZERO WASTE MONEY

One of the ways we can exercise our democratic rights is to vote with our dollar. Teaching your children to be conscious consumers can begin at any age. In order to teach your children about the responsibility of earning and using money, first you'll need to do some self-reflection about your own relationship with money.

When I was growing up my family didn't have much money, but my parents were always financially savvy and lived within their means. When I first came to Sydney, we lived in a poorer part of the city. Our neighborhood was home to many immigrants and low-income families. We weren't destitute, but we were definitely working class. When I was thirteen, I was awarded a scholarship to a prestigious girls' school in Sydney, the kind of school where students wore blazers, knee-high socks, ties and hats. White gloves were also worn on special occasions. I remember catching the train to my new school, blazer too big, with a laptop in my bag that my family couldn't afford, while other girls were being driven to school in Mercedes-Benzes and Porches. It was the first time I realized I was poor.

After this realization I continued to compare my family's wealth to what others had. I felt poor, because I didn't have the "stuff" that would make me look rich. By my early twenties, my relationship with consumerism involved me spending all my money trying to look rich, to mask the sense of inadequacy I had developed from feeling like a poor girl in high school. Since I began living a zero waste life, my relationship with money has totally transformed. I now realize money is a tool for happiness, but it is not the key to happiness.

GIVE, GET, GROW

I want my children to have a better relationship with money than I did, and to instill financial responsibility in them from an early age. Here is a fun way to get started. Upcycle three jars and label them "Give," "Get" and "Grow.

1. **GIVE** – Ask your children to allocate a percentage of their pocket money for giving to others. This is a great way to discuss social issues and people who are in need. Help your children identify a charitable cause they wish to donate to and set a regular interval for making a donation. This might mean once a month, once the jar is full or when it reaches a certain dollar value.

2. **GET** – This money is allocated to getting things your children currently want or need. Encourage them to spend it wisely, not just on stuff, but on experiences and outings too. This is where a conversation about being a conscious consumer in all aspects of their lives is most important. If they want to buy something, encourage them to ask themselves the following questions:

   - Do I really need this item? What are my reasons for wanting to buy it?
   - Can I borrow the item or try it out before I buy it?
   - Can I buy it secondhand?
   - Can I buy it from an ethical brand that aligns with my values?

   These questions will get them really thinking about the root causes of consumption and will help them start changing their mindset about meaningless spending.

3. GROW – This money is set aside to save for a bigger purchase. Watching this jar grow will inspire them to invest and do something meaningful with their long-term savings. Younger children might want to work toward a big purchase such as a bike, or an activity they have been wanting to do for a long time. For older children, this is a good opportunity to discuss investment, particularly buying shares in sustainable industries. You can educate yourselves together and ask questions about where you're currently investing your money as a starting point.

This method doesn't just apply to kids; it's a great way for adults to keep track of their expenditure too. We and our children are inundated with thousands of advertisements on a daily basis. We have been programmed to buy, buy, buy from a young age. Children are also told they aren't cool if they don't have the latest gadget, that they won't fit in without the latest sneakers and that they need to buy their way to popularity and acceptance from their peers. I am sure we can all recall a moment when we were made fun of as a child because we weren't wearing the right clothes or didn't have the latest fad toy. These memories are embedded into us and we compensate as adults by mindlessly consuming. We need to teach our children that they are loved just as they are, and they don't need the latest stuff to be accepted. This begins by fostering confidence in themselves and a good relationship with money from an early age.

ECO, NOT EGO

It's hard for children who live in their small bubbles of home and school to see the bigger picture. As parents, it's natural to want our kids to fit in and have all the best things, and make sure they're not deprived in any way. Our egos are fueled by compliments and acceptance, and peer pressure can be a tricky issue to navigate. Awareness of what is driving our wants is the most important starting point to staunch mindless consumption. With greater awareness, your children will understand that decreased consumption doesn't mean deprivation. In fact, their lives will be fuller when they consume less.

Here are some tips on how to encourage your children to think more broadly.

- VOLUNTEERING – As discussed in Day 20, this will open their eyes to the bigger issues of the world. Volunteer as a family or, if they are older, ask them to commit to something regularly in their own time. Helping someone in need will allow them to "get over themselves" and realize they aren't the center of the world, but rather part of something greater.

• SOCIAL MEDIA BREAKS – Have a screen-free Saturday or Sunday, where the entire family turns off their devices and stores them in the tech bed. Getting away from screens means less exposure to advertising, and less brainwashing to buy, buy, buy.

• SAFE SPACE – Have a family rule that the home is a safe space for your children where they will always be accepted, no matter what happens. This will foster a positive environment for your children to open up about what's bothering them. Having this safe space to ask questions and make mistakes will build their confidence and help them determine where their own morals and values lie.

LET THEM GET DIRTY

My mother always said to me, "All I want is for you to be happy." Now that I'm a parent myself, I understand how genuinely she meant this. This is what all parents want: for our children to always be happy, for everything to turn out fine. The reality is that, despite our best efforts to cushion their blows, bandage their sores and buffer them from the real world, our children will have to get dirty, both literally and metaphorically. We live in an over-sanitized world—there is a soap, wipe and cleanser for every part of the body. Personal hygiene is important, and so is sanitation, but are we taking it too far? The soil in our gardens and parks is full of necessary and helpful bacteria and microbes that are essential to the development of a healthy immune system. There is more and more research being conducted around the benefits of playing in mud and dirt in the development of a healthy gut. Parents nowadays carry around wet wipes, which take hundreds of years to decompose and are wiping away the good bacteria that children need to thrive. We have 99.99 percent bacteria-killing hand soap and home cleaning products that act as a disinfectant to all bacteria, good and bad. There is no doubt that these products are needed in hospitals and nursing homes, and in times of medical need, but let's try to find some zero waste alternatives for use outside of these situations and preserve good bacteria where possible.

CREATE YOUR OWN
ZERO WASTE HANDWASH

Here is a recipe that cleans your hands without drying them out:

- 1 cup castile soap
- 1 cup water
- 1 tablespoon jojoba oil
- 1 tablespoon vitamin E oil
- A few drops of essential oil (my favorites include orange and ylang-ylang).

Combine the ingredients and pour into an upcycled pump bottle.

Another way to reduce your plastic consumption is to use bar soap. This can replace both hand wash and body wash, and you can even switch from bottled shampoo and conditioner to shampoo and conditioning bars.

Letting your children get dirty in the literal sense is important, but we must also allow them to get dirty in the metaphorical sense. This means allowing them controlled exposure to some of the bad parts of the world. It's natural to want to protect them from these things, but children are much more aware than we give them credit for. They are highly sensitive to family dynamics and absorb a lot from their surroundings. I am not suggesting they should see graphic images or violence, but I am encouraging transparency and respect for their intelligence. This means building their awareness to the world around them and the roles they play in it.

Here are some tips on how you can help your children become conscious global citizens without scaring the pants off them.

1. HONESTY – As parents, we often feel the need to use euphemisms or tell elaborate stories when our children ask frank questions. We need to try to train ourselves to be honest and practical, and explain things in simple terms. There's no need to overwhelm your children; the information you provide should be appropriately pitched to their age. Use simple words when explaining problems like plastic pollution or other environmental issues. Be open and straightforward, and encourage them to do their own research, or help them find the answer if you aren't sure. Don't catastrophize the issues, as it will fuel eco-anxiety. Instead, be purposeful and constructive. Always end the discussion by deciding upon a positive action they can take.

2. GETTING OUTSIDE REGULARLY – Enjoying the outdoors and letting your children explore allows them to see for themselves

what all this eco-conscious effort is for. Let them experience forests, mountains, parks, beaches, rivers and lakes. Don't be afraid to let them be curious and adventurous. Accept the fact that they will be getting dirty and that there will be more laundry to be done. Don't let your rules for cleanliness overshadow their natural urge to explore nature.

3. **NURTURING SOMETHING** – Give your children responsibility for something, be it a plant, a garden bed or a pet. Watching something grow, nurturing it day to day and then reaping the rewards is such a worthwhile experience. It will teach them about patience, hard work and the wonder of the natural world.

4. **MAKE IT** – Many of the zero waste recipes in this book (and also in *A Zero Waste Life*) can be made by or with children. The ingredients are simple and there is minimal effort required. This is a great way to teach your children important life skills. As they get older, you could work on a project together such as upcycling and repainting old furniture or creating something from scratch by sewing or cooking.

5. **CHANGE YOUR LANGUAGE** – We've all been there: the shouty parent saying "Don't" and "No" when we're worried for our child's safety. By yelling out such negative commands we are teaching our kids to be afraid of nature. Instead of fearing every bump, scrape and fall, why not change your language to be more encouraging and welcoming. Start with positive verbs, or do something together to alleviate your and their fears.

TAKE THREE
FOR THE SEA

Whenever you are at the seaside, don't forget to #take3forthesea. This is a wonderful campaign to encourage people to pick up and dispose of at least three pieces of trash whenever they are at the beach. This simple task is a practical, hands-on way to make a small difference, but most importantly, it opens kids' eyes to the plastic in our waterways. You could even make it a game to see who can collect the most pieces of trash!

CREATE A CAPSULE WARDROBE FOR YOUR CHILDREN

Wanting to look good is not a sin. Style is a way for children to express themselves creatively. We should not be slaves to fashion, and nor should we fund slave labor to produce fast fashion, but style is something that should be embraced. There's a certain snobbery in the environmental world that you have to reject the idea of dressing nicely and look the part of a hippie-activist to actually be an environmental activist. I want to introduce you to the modern-day activist. They look just like you and me, but make careful decisions about where they invest their money. If you love good style, don't let that go, just make some sensible switches. This also applies to your children: don't discourage their enthusiasm for fashion as superficial or not compatible with a zero waste lifestyle; instead, encourage them to be inspired, not influenced.

Here are some ways to create a capsule wardrobe for your children of all ages.

INFANTS

Buy bulk secondhand clothing that is age and season appropriate. Choose clothing that can be machine washed and is durable. At this age, clothing should be practical—functionality is the key. Some of my essentials for my daughter included seven to ten zip-up onesies, which made dressing simple and easy. Nighttime changes were also a breeze. For winter, add three to five jumpers or cardigans in neutral colors, which can be layered over the onesie. They should be good quality jumpers with a wide body and sleeves, which allows them to stretch and be layered easily.

TODDLERS

Choose colors that suit your child and pieces that they can easily mix and match. I like to have easy layering pieces and create a small wardrobe that includes:

- five short-sleeved T-shirts
- five long-sleeved shirts
- three jumpers or cardigans
- three pairs of shorts for summer
- three pairs of pants for winter
- one winter jacket
- five pairs of socks.

These pieces should suffice for a toddler's everyday wear. You might also like to add one or two special occasion outfits to suit your lifestyle. I apply the one in, one out rule for my children's clothes as well. This prevents the accrual of excessive clothing and saves you time in the morning when putting together outfits.

SCHOOL-AGED CHILDREN

Create a capsule wardrobe for school-aged children with seven outfits that they love and can mix and match. Involve them in the process of creating the capsule wardrobe. Spend an afternoon cutting out pictures and colors from magazines, or create an online inspiration board on Pinterest. This is a great way to see what your children are interested in, who their role models are and what inspires them. It's rare that we sit down with our children and discuss who their heroes are and why they want to emulate them. Encourage them to think about the reasons why they think this person is cool, and discuss their positive attributes.

Once you've developed an inspiration board, spend a couple of weekends sourcing outfits together from secondhand stores or markets. This is a great bonding activity and it's a fun way to get your creativity flowing. Have fun with accessories, experiment with colors and don't be afraid to try new things. This experience will take both of you out of your comfort zones and provide an opportunity to try new things.

TEENAGERS

This is the age where influencing your kids' wardrobe can be tricky, because teens rarely want parental input on their fashion choices. However, you can still set a challenge for them, such as curating a thirty-piece capsule wardrobe. Don't be afraid to be adventurous together. As with your school-aged children, create an inspiration board of who they want to look like and how they want to dress. Don't judge their decisions; rather, see it as a creative process that allows them to open up to you. If they gravitate toward large logos and designer labels, ask them why they chose those items, and talk about whether they might be feeling the influence of marketing and consumerism rather than embracing true style. If they still like the style of something, brainstorm how they can replicate the look with secondhand finds. After that, if they still want to wear a particular designer or brand, encourage them to save for it or find a way to make some extra money to earn it.

If they are embarrassed to be seen in secondhand stores, encourage them to shop secondhand online. You can make informed purchases together. The teenage years are the time to start educating your children on the fast fashion industry and the billion-dollar beauty industry. Have open discussions about the marketing behind these industries, much of which is designed to make us feel insecure or inferior. Don't lecture them, just be open. Share your own experiences with how consumption of more stuff wasn't the key to making you feel more beautiful, or giving you more confidence.

WARDROBE WORKOUT

This idea is inspired by my friend Faye De Lanty, who is an eco-stylist and has a successful Instagram account, @fayedelanty. She runs a weekly series called "Wardrobe Workout," where she collects images from the latest runway shows, or celebrities who inspire her, and replicates the outfit with items she already has in her wardrobe. She challenges other people to do the same and has done collaborations with many social media influencers, myself included. Her creative flair is truly inspirational. She transforms items she already owns into runway-quality looks, all with the clever placement of a brooch, scarf or belt. We can do this with our children's wardrobes. Make it a fun family activity! You can be as serious or as frivolous as you like. It's like playing dress-up, but with a purpose. Your children will feel so inspired afterward. You could even take pictures of the outfits as if you're at a magazine shoot, or create a runway parade.

ZERO WASTE DIET

Cooking for children can be an elaborate affair. In a lot of households, we succumb to convenience foods because we simply don't have the time. This often means buying packaged, processed foods that are not only unhealthy for you and your children, but are also detrimental to the planet.

I would like to suggest a new way of thinking about food. I call it being a "template chef." The template chef takes basic recipes and mixes and matches the ingredients according to what is in season, what they have in their pantry and what needs to be eaten to avoid food waste. I've created cooking templates for my favorite meals, which you can easily adapt. You can also get your children involved in the kitchen and get them to help too.

All the recipes below are for one serving; scale them up to suit your family size.

TEMPLATE CHEF RECIPES: BREAKFAST

I cycle through these recipes for breakfast every day. They are simple, zero waste and easy to fit into a quick morning routine.

THE BIG BREAKFAST – ONE PORTION

Protein: eggs – 2	Beans – 1/2 cup
	Vegetable – 1/2 cup – 1 1/2 cups

This is a simple zero waste recipe that you can adapt according to what is in season. If you stick to this template, your children will be full for hours.

- Eggs: these are a healthy source of protein. Make sure you buy free range and from a local source if possible.
- Beans: buy these in dried form from the bulk store and soak overnight to rehydrate. They are an excellent source of fiber.
- Vegetables: choose what is in season, which provides variety!

Here are some examples of different adaptions of this template.

SIMPLE BIG BREAKFAST

| 2 folded eggs | ½ cup red kidney beans |
| | ½ cup broccoli |

BAKED EGGS

| 2 eggs | ½ cup cannellini beans |
| | ½ can diced tomatoes |

Add the beans and diced tomatoes to an oven-safe ramekin, then make a well in the center of the mixture and crack the eggs into the well. Bake in the oven at 400 degrees Fahrenheit until eggs are cooked, about 8–12 minutes.

BREAKFAST SALAD

| 2 boiled eggs, sliced | ½ cup chickpeas |
| | 1½ cups salad greens |

Mix together with a simple dressing of your choice.

As you can see, the template is the same, but the options are endless. You can increase the portion sizes according to your family's needs and add sauces and condiments (bought in glass jars or home-made) according to what you like. But the most important thing is that there is minimal thinking involved.

RICH MAN'S PORRIDGE

1 cup oats	½ cup poached seasonal fruit
	1 cup nut or oat milk

I call this rich man's porridge because you can make it as luxe as you like!

- Oats: buy them from the bulk store, and be adventurous with the different types of oats available.
- Poached seasonal fruit: think mangoes and peaches in summer, pears and apples in winter.
- Nut or oat milk: this can be store-bought, of course, but I like to make my own, and it is so simple. I have some easy nut milk recipes on the next page.

POACHED FRUIT

An easy way to poach fruit is to put it in a slow cooker and cook on low for 8 hours, or on high for 4 hours. I do this once a week, then store the fruit in glass containers and dish it out for breakfast.

HOMEMADE NUT MILK

Low waste option—this is one of my favorite life hacks! Just buy a jar of your favorite nut butter, combine 2 tablespoons of nut butter and 1 liter of water in a high-speed blender, and blend away for simple, no-mess nut milk! This will last for three days in the refrigerator if stored in a sealed jar.

Zero waste option—soak 1 cup of raw, unsalted nuts overnight. Drain away the water, then blend the soaked nuts with 1 liter of water until smooth. Strain with a nut milk bag or muslin cloth. It will last in the refrigerator for three days.

HOMEMADE OAT MILK

Add 1 cup of rolled oats, 1 liter of water, 2 pitted dates and a pinch of salt to a high-speed blender. Blend for 30–45 seconds. Strain with a nut milk bag or muslin cloth. It should last for up to five days in the refrigerator.

CHIA SEED PUDDING

	Fruit, nuts, dates
½ cup chia seeds	½ cup nut or oat milk

This is such a simple recipe, but you can be creative with it! Just add a
1 : 1 ratio of chia seeds and oat or nut milk then mix in some chopped
fruit, nuts or dates. Let the mixture sit overnight in the refrigerator
in some cups or small jars, and you have an easy chia seed pudding!
This is a great recipe for when you have no time to prepare food in
the morning and need something you can easily grab from the fridge.
They are also great afternoon snacks for kids.

TEMPLATE CHEF RECIPES: LUNCH

THE FRIENDLY SALAD

	Roasted seasonal vegetables
Palm-sized portion of protein	
	2 cups salad leaves

There's a great episode of *The Simpsons* with an unforgettable jingle that says "You can't make friends with salad." I've named this recipe the friendly salad, because you *can* make friends with salad!

This is my go-to lunch for the whole family.

- Protein: if you're a meat-eater, choose sustainably sourced chicken, turkey, fish or other meat. Remember to take your own containers to the butcher and ask them to fill those instead of putting the meat in plastic bags.

- Vegetables: jazz up your roasted vegetables by adding a homemade honey glaze, or add different spices, which you can get from the bulk store.

- Salad leaves: don't forget to bring your own produce bags for loose salad leaves, and store them in airtight glass containers when you get home to extend the life of the leaves.

This salad can be built upon with nuts, seeds and different homemade salad dressings.

THE BENTO BOX

Palm-sized portion of protein	Steamed seasonal vegetables
	1 cup cooked rice

This is a great lunch recipe for children, and you can invest in a stainless steel bento box to make it even more fun!

- Protein: sustainably sourced fish such as sardines or tuna are a great option. Marinate them in a soy sauce to make it even more delicious!
- Steamed vegetables: you can use a small cookie cutter to make fun shapes out of steamed vegetables to make it seem more like a Japanese bento box.
- Rice: experiment with different types of rice from the bulk food store, such as wild rice, brown rice and jasmine rice. Add sesame seeds, coconut oil, saffron or a splash of soy sauce to make it more interesting.

PASTA SALAD

Palm-sized portion of protein	Roasted seasonal vegetables
	1 cup cooked pasta

The key to pasta salads is to change up the dressing or sauce to keep the meal interesting and fresh. My favorite is whole-egg mayonnaise or basil pesto.

WHOLE EGG MAYONNAISE

Mix together 2 eggs, 2 tablespoons of lemon juice, ½ tablespoon of salt, ½ teaspoon of white pepper and 2 cups of vegetable oil in a high-speed blender. This can refrigerate well for 2–3 weeks.

JAGESY'S BASIL PESTO

My friend Danielle (Jagesy) taught me this recipe when I was sixteen and ever since then I have made it at least once a week. Add 1 large bunch of fresh basil, ¼ cup of roasted pine nuts (or any nut that you have), ½ cup of olive oil, grated Parmesan (optional) and salt and pepper to taste to a food processor and blitz until the pesto forms a chunky paste. This will last for 1 week when refrigerated.

TEMPLATE CHEF RECIPES: DINNER

SLOW CURRY

| Palm-sized portion of protein | Seasonal vegetables – choose whatever is in season and dice into small pieces (it all tastes good in this curry) |
| | 1–2 tablespoons of your favorite curry paste + 1 cup coconut milk |

Mix together a diced raw protein, chopped seasonal vegetables, some of your favorite curry paste (or make your own) and a cup of coconut milk. Put this in a slow cooker in the morning on low and it will be ready for dinner (approximately 8 hours cooking time). You can also cook this on a stovetop for 45 minutes to one hour.

SHIRLEY'S NOODLE SOUP

| 1 serving of noodles | Asian greens |
| | Diced cooked protein |

My mom (Shirley) would make this soup for me after a long day at school and it was such a healing and comforting part of the day. Choose your favorite noodles from the bulk store, or try Asian grocers to get fresh noodles which you take home in your own container. Add the noodles to a pot with 1 liter of boiling water, then add in a miso concentrate or vegetable broth (which can both be bought in glass jars). Boil until the noodles are cooked then add in your protein of choice and also Asian greens to warm through. Flavor with sesame oil, chili oil, soy sauce or chili sauce. All of these items can be found at your local Asian grocer in glass containers.

LEFTOVER FRITTATA

This is something I make on the night before my organic produce box is being delivered. I take all the vegetables out of my "eat first" box in the fridge, dice them up and mix them together with 8–10 lightly beaten eggs. I then pour the mixture into a round pan and cook it in the oven at 400 degrees Fahrenheit for 20 minutes. Make a salad to go with it and you have an easy meal that also saves food from going to a landfill.

ZERO WASTE SCHOOL

The beginning of the school year is punctuated by back-to-school sales. It can be a time of year where you pile shopping carts full of plastic-wrapped items, only a handful of which might ever get used. Schools send out a shopping list and, as good parents, we promptly buy everything suggested without a second thought. There's no getting away from it—school requires "stuff," but here are some ideas for making back-to-school more eco-friendly.

BAGS, UNIFORMS AND SPORTS GEAR

My mom and I would always visit the secondhand uniform store at the beginning of the year. I went to a private school, and the uniform alone cost more than my mom made in a week. I had no shame in buying secondhand because no one else knew. That's the joy of buying secondhand: often, no one would know unless you told them. If your children have qualms about wearing secondhand clothes, explain to them that all clothing items, even "new" ones, have been handled by many people before they come into your wardrobe. Having worked in retail for years, I know firsthand how many people have handled an item of clothing before it ends up in the store, and even after that, how many people try on a garment before you buy it. Explain this to your children so they understand the product life cycle and can see that secondhand isn't second best.

Buying a bag is a worthwhile investment. As always, invest in the best quality you can afford and it'll last a lot longer than a cheaper sportswear bag. If you don't have the budget to buy new, look for quality items you can pick up secondhand.

Sports gear can get very expensive when you factor in the cost of uniforms, equipment, bags and training gear. If your children are playing a sport for just one term, or taking some trial lessons, ask to borrow equipment from the school or from friends before you go out and buy anything. Many people have unused tennis rackets, hockey sticks and large sports bags that sit unused in closets and garages. Only invest in quality items if your children decide to play the sport for longer than a few weeks.

SCHOOL SUPPLIES

Today there are so many great options for zero waste school supplies. Here are some tips to make the choices easier for you.

- **PAPER PRODUCTS** – Choose paper products that have a recycled content and don't have plastic covers, wire binding or any materials that can't be easily recycled.

- **PENS** – Use what you have first! Many of us have too many pens and pencils tucked away in our drawers. Use what you have before you buy anything new. In choosing new products, select items that can be reused, such as refillable ink pens.

- **HIGHLIGHTERS** – Did you know that there are such things as highlighter pencils? Do your research and see if you can find items that are made from wood or can be refilled rather than ones made of disposable plastic.

- **MAKE YOUR OWN** – I love making my own notepads using the back of one-sided printed pages. I use the blank side and then recycle the paper afterward, extending the life of the resource. These recycled notebooks are suitable for grocery shopping lists, doodling or taking notes.

- **RULERS, ART SUPPLIES AND OTHER ITEMS** — Source as much as possible of what you need secondhand. Have a look on Facebook swap groups, or talk to other parents at your children's school about whether they would be interested in setting up a real-life swap. Remember, many people know they have too much stuff and would be grateful for someone to take it off their hands.

- **USE IT UP FIRST** — Notebooks are notebooks, so resist the temptation of shiny new things and use notebooks cover to cover before you buy another one. Simply rip out the pages that have already been used to get a fresh start. You can freshen up the cover with some decoupage or wrapping paper if they are worn out or if your children's interests have changed. Folders can also be given a new lease on life by covering them in high-quality wrapping paper. Pencil cases can be sourced secondhand from thrift stores, and lots of small bags and cosmetics bags can make great pencil cases too. Get creative with what you have and make it a fun task for your children to find something unique.

LUNCHES

- **INVEST IN AN INSULATED THERMOS FOR EACH CHILD** – These are wonderful for keeping soups warm, but they can also keep salads fresh and leftovers hot.

- **ASK FOR FEEDBACK** – Do your children prefer sandwiches or salads? If apples come home uneaten, is it because they don't like them, or maybe because they're difficult to chew? If it's the latter, you could try slicing and peeling the apples to make them easier to eat. Ask for constructive feedback so that all the food gets eaten and you're not wasting food or money.

- **MAKE IT LOOK NICE** – Invest in a bento box to neatly display school snacks and lunches. Garnish the food with herbs, nuts, seeds and spices. Slice or cut up fruit using cookie cutters. Making a meal look appealing will encourage kids to eat it all!

- **MAKE YOUR OWN KID-SIZED SNACKS** – Individually wrapped "kid-sized" servings are a waste of money and come with excessive plastic packaging. Buy nuts, dried fruit, crackers, hummus, fruit or carrot sticks in bulk and make your own single servings of it. I like to use washable silicone bags or small jars for individual portions.

- **BUY AN INSULATED REUSABLE DRINK BOTTLE** – These are great to keep drinks cold for the summer months and warm in winter. Choose an appropriately sized drink bottle and make it easy for your children to drink out of by choosing the right sipper or reusable straw. You can flavor the water with fruit for a treat.

- **INVEST IN A ZERO WASTE LUNCH KIT** – This includes a reusable cutlery set and also a cloth napkin for wiping the face and hands. The cloth napkin can also be used to store any leftover dry foods, such as cookies or nuts.

ZERO WASTE HABITS

There are many elements of our homes that we take for granted and can overlook when we are making an effort to reduce our waste. My grandfather grew up in China at a time when people were very careful about their electricity use. I remember he would turn off all the lights as soon as he left a room, and would bark at everyone else to do the same. He was equally vigilant about electrical appliances—if it wasn't being used, he would unplug it. He was so militant about conserving electricity that he would even turn off the lights while we were still in the room. It was a running family joke that we would be in the middle of dinner and all of a sudden it would be pitch black because my grandfather had left the room.

This mindset of conservation, resourcefulness and thriftiness is something many of us don't have to think about. We take for granted the availability of clean water, free-flowing electricity and unpolluted air. Encouraging a zero waste mindset from an early age starts with changing our daily habits. Here are some ways the entire family can get involved in establishing zero waste habits.

ZERO WASTE ELECTRICITY

Unprecedented bushfires ravaged Australia in the summer of 2019–2020. Australians were asked to reduce their electricity usage on the hottest days to prevent overloading powerlines, which could trigger bushfires. Even outside of emergency situations like that, electricity consumption can be expensive and, in many countries, fossil fuels are still used to generate electricity. So let's conserve electricity and treat it like the precious resource it is.

Here are some simple, practical ways to reduce your electricity usage, wherever you are in the world.

1. **SWITCH IT OFF** – Turn off any electronics that are not in use and unplug them or switch them off at the power point—many electrical appliances draw low levels of electricity even when they are not being used. Ask your children to do the same, to help them develop this mindful habit.

2. **LIGHTS OFF** – Hold an "earth hour" before bed. Earth Hour is an international event held once a year, where households and businesses switch off their lights from 8–9 p.m. to save electricity. There's no reason you can't do it more than once a year by switching off all the lights in your house and lighting some candles for ambiance and low light (but always be sensible with open flames).

3. **TURN OFF THE AIR CONDITIONER AND USE A FAN INSTEAD** –
   During summer, use a fan in the evenings and save the air
   conditioning for the hottest part of the day. Try misting your skin
   with ice water in a spray bottle on hot days.

4. **TURN OFF THE HEATING** – Try to reduce your use of heaters and
   air-conditioning in the colder months. When I traveled in Iceland,
   I learned a wonderful expression: "There is no such thing as bad
   weather, there is only bad clothing and a bad attitude." This has
   become my ethos for when anyone in my family complains about
   the weather. If it's cold, instead of jumping to turn on the heater,
   put on warmer clothing and socks. Thermals also do wonders
   and are a great investment. You can use warmer bedding in the
   evening as well. I have a wool blanket covering my duvet in winter
   and it helps insulate the heat. It has proven to be a worthwhile
   investment.

5. **AIR-DRY INSIDE** – Avoid the clothes dryer and air-dry all your
   clothes. If the weather is poor outside, consider purchasing a
   clothes airer that can be used indoors.

ZERO WASTE WATER

Much of Australia has been in drought since 2017—the ongoing world-wide climate crisis has resulted in one of the worst droughts in the nation's history. Drought also affects places like California, and Cape Town, South Africa. In recent years, Cape Town has been on the brink of total water shortages, with the situation so dire they have come up with a name for the day when the water will completely run out—"Day Zero." Cape Town residents have taken drastic measures to reduce their water consumption, and this collective effort is working.

Without fresh, clean drinking water, there is no life. Let's conserve this precious resource and make sure it is not wasted. Here are some easy water-saving measures you can adopt.

1. **PUT A BUCKET IN YOUR SHOWER** – This will capture excess water that you can use to water your plants. Just make sure the soap you use is plant friendly.

2. **SAVE YOUR COOKING WATER** – If you're boiling vegetables, eggs or pasta, save the water, allow it to cool and use it to water your garden! The nutrients from the food will seep into the water and provide your plants with a boost similar to compost or fertilizer.

3. **SAVE GRAY WATER FOR YOUR GARDEN** – Gray water includes things such as washing-up water, bath water and laundry water. You can save it and use it to water the garden, or to flush your toilet.

4. **TAKE THREE-MINUTE SHOWERS** – The shorter your shower can be, the better! Set a timer and try your best to keep to the three-minute rule. Instead of a timer, your children could choose their favorite song under three minutes and make sure they finish their shower before the song ends. Why not get everyone in the family involved and make it a fun competition?

5. **CHOOSE REUSABLE INSTEAD OF DISPOSABLE** – Many of the materials we use every day, such as plastic and textiles, require a huge amount of water to process and manufacture. If you choose secondhand or reusable options, you're preventing the need for virgin materials to be consumed.

ZERO WASTE GASOLINE

Think of all the activities in your life that require a car. Many of them likely involve chauffeuring your children from one engagement to another. Here are some simple ideas to reduce your gasoline consumption. They will help remind everyone in the family that gas is expensive and comes from fossil fuels, so we need to minimize our use of it.

1. **EMBRACE ACTIVE TRANSPORT** – Think walking, running, cycling or even using a scooter. Especially if you only need to travel a short distance, try these forms of transport instead of immediately jumping in the car.

2. **CHOOSE PUBLIC TRANSPORT** – Taking the bus, subway or train is an adventure in itself. Young children especially love public transport, so try these options instead of taking the car. It'll also save money spent on parking.

3. **GROUP YOUR ERRANDS** – Have you noticed that your family needs to dash to the shops almost every day? Someone has forgotten to buy milk, another needs pens for school, and then you're back again the next day because you've run out of bread! The command station is a great way to organize your family's time. Keep an ongoing list of errands to be run on the command station, such as the supermarket visit, bulk store visit, post office visit, bank visit and so on, and group them together based on location. If you need to go to the supermarket and the post office is next door, make sure you run those errands together.

4. **CARPOOL** – When you are traveling to group activities, suggest a rotating carpool system to reduce the number of cars making the trip. When I was on the cricket team in high school, we had a rotating schedule of parents who could drive team members to different events. Instead of being a personal chauffeur to all of your children's activities, share the load and start a carpool roster.

THE GOLDEN TRIANGLE PRINCIPLE

Researchers have proposed the "golden triangle" principle, which states that the optimal level of happiness can be found when your home, work and leisure activities are all within a two-mile area. This is a happy walking distance that reduces the length of commutes and averts road rage, and helps form a sense of connection with your local neighborhood. I have chosen to live in a 635-square-foot home with my family so I can recreate this golden triangle rule, and it's made my life infinitely happier. The fact I can walk to work, the shops and the local park has made my life much less stressful, and it has also embedded me as part of the community. You might not be able to recreate this exact golden triangle for yourself, but think about how you can optimize your commute so that you spend less time traveling and more time living.

SHARE IN THE COMMONS

How many of us know our neighbors? Interact with our produce vendors? Know the names of the people who make our clothing? I remember when I was growing up in China, everyone knew each other on the street where we lived. The whole neighborhood knew my grandparents, because my grandfather ran a telephone stand for the street. There was a printing press next door and a childcare provider down the road. Further along the street was a wet market for fresh meat and a produce market in the local square. My grandfather was a stoic man—he didn't say much—but when he was taking me for our daily walk, he would stop and talk to everyone. He took great pride in being part of the community.

Coming to Australia, the greatest difference I noticed (at the ripe old age of four) was that no one spoke to each other. No one greeted us in the street, stopped to say hello or dropped in for some tea. The only family I had was my immediate family. It was a lonely existence. In Australia, I felt materially wealthier but poorer for the loss of our community.

The term "commons" comes from the traditional English legal term for common land, or shared land that everyone was allowed to access. I'm using it here to mean our communities and all the shared resources within them. This includes people who look out for each other and for children in the community, people who respect water and the land on which they live because they know it has to be shared, and the sense of collective spirit that we are all part of something bigger. Along the way society has sacrificed the commons to make way for common wealth. We are individually richer than we've ever been in history, but we are in many ways spiritually poorer for it.

START WITH A ZERO WASTE MINDSET

Sharing in the commons is an obvious way you can lead by example and demonstrate how to live a truly zero waste life. In sharing our resources, we are inherently preventing waste by using everything to its fullest capacity. A zero waste mindset means that we can all be zero waste engineers and artists; we can all engage in creative problem-solving to find collective solutions. It encourages teamwork, resilience and working toward a common goal.

Today is a day to share in the commons and embrace being part of the community again. Here are some simple ways to encourage this new mindset for you and your family.

1. **DON'T BE AFRAID OF YOUR NEIGHBORS** – If you don't know your neighbors, get to know them! Say hello when you see them out and about. Invite them over for a cup of tea and conversation. We live in a world where we've become fearful of strangers—let's see what happens when we try to be more open.

2. **CONTRIBUTE TO YOUR COMMUNITY** – See if you can spend a few hours a month volunteering and getting to know others in the community. This could be at your local community garden or at a charity shop, or you could form a neighborhood group for an environmental event like National CleanUp Day. Organize a block party for your street. Don't be afraid to be the instigator of a great plan.

3. **SUPPORT LOCAL BUSINESS OWNERS** – I avoid large supermarkets and shopping centers as much as possible, and choose to buy most of my produce from local businesses. The costs are almost the same, but the relationships you develop are priceless. I love that when I walk around my neighborhood, everyone knows me and I know them.

4. **VISIT LOCAL PARKS** – Take advantage of all the green spots around you and walk to them on a regular basis. Give yourself a daily "green prescription" to visit a local park. There's a great activity that originated in Sweden called "plogging," which

combines jogging with picking up trash. Whenever you are going for a run or a jog, pick up some pieces of trash that are lying around and dispose of them thoughtfully. I've even put some gardening gloves in my pocket before I head out for a run as a reminder to pick up trash when I see it. Ask your children to do the same.

5. **USE YOUR LOCAL LIBRARY** – My local library is a hive of activity and the center of the community. It runs so many programs and events for young and old. One of my favorite memories is watching my daughter at rhyme time for 0–2-year-olds at the library, and seeing other people without children come and join in the fun.

6. **FREE ACTIVITIES** – When I lived in San Francisco, they had free swimming lessons for babies under five months. National parks and botanical gardens often have free activities for children like sensory experiences or lessons about wildlife. Check out the websites of public and cultural institutions near you, and sign up to newsletters that list what's available in your city. Museums, opera houses, concert halls and music venues all have free activities for children too. There's no need to spend hundreds of dollars on amusement parks when there are so many free activities near our homes.

FIJI TIME

In 2016, I spent two weeks volunteering my skills as a medical student in Suva, Fiji. My memories of that time that have lingered aren't the stereotypical images of Fiji—white sandy beaches, endless cocktails and great nightclubs—it's actually what the locals call "Fiji time."

"Fiji time" is a reminder that things don't need to start exactly on time. It is an appreciation for a slower-paced life. I remember walking with one of the Fijian students to the local town. It was a trip that might have taken fifteen minutes, but instead it took us two hours. This is because he stopped and talked to everyone that he knew. Whenever he heard a "bula," a greeting of hello with a wish for wellness, we stopped and chatted with the person, asked about their day and their family. If we bumped into that same person again, we would do the same thing even if we had just spoken ten minutes earlier. This strong sense of community really resonated with me. It made me feel special that people took time out of their busy days to stop and ask about me. We all need to slow down and smell the roses, otherwise we are rushing to our graves. Let's embrace a bit of Fiji time in our everyday lives.

ZERO WASTE HOBBIES

Hobbies, crafts and games help pass the time on a rainy day, but they can also be family activities that encourage learning and creativity! As parents, we can be tempted to rush out and buy the latest gadget to entertain our children. However, I want to show you that keeping your children occupied doesn't have to mean buying more stuff, especially when so much of this stuff is packaged in plastic.

GARDENING

A fun hobby that the whole family can enjoy is starting a garden using materials you already have at home.

- **GROW A GARDEN FROM YOUR FOOD SCRAPS** – So many food scraps that you would normally compost can be regrown into a plant. An avocado seed can be regrown by piercing it with four toothpicks, then using them to rest the seed over the opening of a glass jar and filling it with water until the seed is about halfway submerged. Bok choy can be regrown by retaining the base in a shallow container of water until new leaves appear. Green onions can also produce new shoots if the bulbs are placed in water. Do some research on how you can regrow your family's favorite vegetables from food scraps.

- **SEED POTS** – Cardboard milk or juice cartons make excellent small planter boxes. Just lay the carton on its side, cut out one of the long sides and make some drainage holes in the opposite side, then fill with soil and plant seeds or seedlings. Reuse old egg cartons and toilet paper rolls that you can fill with soil and add some seeds. These act as great seedling punnets, which you can then transfer to larger planters as they grow.

- **MAKE YOUR OWN WATERING CAN** – You can reuse plastic bottles and make them into watering cans for children. Use a hammer and nail to poke a few holes in the lid of the bottle, then fill it with water (ideally from one of the water-saving ideas discussed in Day 26). Kids will have so much fun squeezing the bottles to create a gentle shower of water, which is also perfect for watering plants.

DO-IT-YOURSELF

There are an abundance of child-friendly zero waste DIYs. This is a fun way to encourage children young and old to get involved in making products that are environmentally friendly and useful for the whole household. You can make cleaning products, beauty products and many other items that can be used at school and around the home. Here are two project ideas to get you started.

HOMEMADE PLAY-DOH

- 1 cup plain flour
- 1 cup water
- 1/4 cup salt
- 1 tablespoon vegetable oil
- 1–2 teaspoons food coloring.

Add all the ingredients except the food coloring to a saucepan and stir over low to medium heat for about five minutes. When the mixture forms a ball, remove the pan from the heat and let it cool. Once it is cool enough to handle, add the food coloring and knead with your hands until the dough becomes smooth. This activity requires supervision for younger children, but you can get them involved in choosing the colors and kneading the mixture.

REUSABLE BEESWAX WRAPS

Beeswax wraps are a great alternative to cling wrap or plastic food wrapping, and they make excellent zero waste gifts. This activity is suited to older children who can safely handle the hot iron. You need:

- 100 percent cotton fabric (source this from secondhand stores, or use old T-shirts or linen you have in your home)
- grated pure beeswax (you can often find this at farmers' markets, or buy online)
- clothing iron
- an old towel
- nonstick baking paper.

Prewash the fabric to prevent it from shrinking, and cut it to your desired size—25 x 25 cm squares is a good starting point. Preheat the iron to a low–medium heat with the steam setting turned off. Lay the old towel down on a flat, hard surface and then place a piece of baking paper larger than the size of your fabric cut-outs with a piece of fabric on top. Sprinkle a little grated beeswax evenly over the fabric (you don't need to use much as it will melt and spread). Start with less and add more if needed. Cover with another sheet of baking paper larger than the fabric and then iron over the baking paper. The wax will melt and soak into the fabric. Carefully lift the baking paper and add more grated wax to any uncoated areas, then cover and iron again until the entire fabric is coated in wax. Hang to cool and dry.

EXERCISE

To encourage a regular and healthy fitness routine, create zero waste exercise habits that don't require a gym membership or any expensive new equipment.

1. **MOVE DAILY** – Incidental exercise is a great way to encourage children to move (without them even knowing it). Consider leaving the car at home and walking to school, the local park or your local shops, or simply parking further away from your destination. This might mean parking a couple of blocks away or at the far end of the car park. Also make an effort to take the stairs instead of the elevator whenever possible to increase your cardio workout and decrease your electricity usage at the same time.

2. **INVEST IN A FEW KEY (SECONDHAND) ITEMS** – Look at simple home gym solutions that you can purchase secondhand. Invest in a good quality yoga mat, jump rope, weights or whatever exercise equipment your family will actually use and enjoy. Exercising in a home gym can be a fun family bonding activity. You can assign each family member a day of the week to be the personal trainer and set that day's workout. Young children can recreate aerobic exercises, dance routines or games they have learned at school, and older children can devise a routine or organize a yoga or Pilates session with the use of online videos. There are many free exercise apps and online resources to help get you moving, so do some research as a family to find out what activities suit you.

3. **FAMILY CHALLENGES** – If creating a home gym isn't suitable for your home or family, consider doing a fitness challenge together instead. This could mean working toward a community running event such as a 5-kilometer walk or a 10-kilometer fun run. Adapt the goal to suit your family's fitness aims. Another option could be challenging each family member to walk at least 10,000 steps a day and charting everyone's progress on the home command station. You don't need to invest in an expensive fitness watch for this; a mechanical pedometer that costs a few dollars will suffice.

FUN-
CYCLE

Zero waste hobbies enable your children to be creative with the resources they already have. We want to encourage them to be materialists in the truest sense of the word, meaning that they value the material that their products are made from. Nothing needs to be seen as waste. Items in the recycling bin can be transformed into zero waste craft materials. Used boxes, discarded milk crates and wooden boxes can be building blocks for a homemade fort or cubbyhouse. Old sheets can be used for dress-ups or for sewing projects. The options are endless: just inject some creativity into fun-cycling.

ZERO WASTE EVERY DAY

As the end of our thirty-day zero waste journey approaches, it is time to reflect on the changes you have made as a family. It is said that it takes thirty days to change a habit, and I hope this journey has opened your eyes to the benefits of living a truly zero waste life. Today is the day to take stock of all your successes and also your missteps, to see what worked and what didn't. An agenda for this day could be:

1. Hold a family meeting to discuss the changes that have occurred. Schedule it at your command station and in your calendars.
2. Make sure everyone has the chance to speak about their experiences. Start with giving everyone the opportunity to talk about their highs and lows from the past thirty days.
3. Brainstorm the benefits and challenges, and possible solutions to these challenges.

To aid you in your brainstorming session, I've put together a list of common benefits, challenges and solutions to living a zero waste life. Become a zero waste engineer and add to and adapt these solutions to make sustainable living sustainable for you.

BECOME A ZERO WASTE ENGINEER

Becoming a zero waste engineer is about finding solutions to problems. It is important to listen to each of the concerns that your family members raise, but, equally, it's important to not just complain but to try to find solutions. A zero waste engineer uses creativity, ingenuity and intelligence to tackle each problem. This is an added benefit of embarking on this lifestyle change: it encourages you and your family to be innovative and think outside the (plastic) box.

BENEFITS

More quality time spent together as a family	Saves money!
Fewer chores to do	More free time
Fewer unwanted distractions	More time for creative pursuits
Getting to know our neighbors	Discovering our local community
Living in alignment with our values	Feeling empowered to make the world a better place

CHALLENGES AND SOLUTIONS

Challenge	Solution
People might judge us	Transform this to, "We are leaders." Not everyone is going to understand your lifestyle changes, and you don't need everyone to understand. The people who ask about it in a curious manner will be the ones who you can inspire to make a change. Don't try to convert anyone, just do your own thing. There is a saying that goes, "Integrity is doing the right thing even when no one is watching." You and your family must have strong intrinsic reasons for wanting to live a zero waste life. It is a way to do something positive for the environment, and it is a form of everyday activism to help make this world a better place. Your values are reflected in your actions, and there is nothing more powerful than living in alignment with your values.

It takes more effort to do things	Transform this to, "Once this becomes a habit, I won't even notice the effort." Admittedly, making any change in your life takes effort. But, as with exercise, if you repeat the same task again and again, muscle memory forms and it becomes second nature. I've been living a zero waste lifestyle for more than six years now, and it has become second nature. I don't even think about the effort anymore. It's actually less effort than my previous lifestyle, because I am living mindfully and minimally.
I miss our screens	Transform this to, "We have more freedom." Silicon Valley tech entrepreneurs have gone on record saying that they are aiming to reduce their screen time as much as possible. They know firsthand how addictive and draining screens can be. Discuss with your children the benefits of being outdoors more, giving themselves freedom to be more creative, and allowing their minds to rest.

I want to fit in and just be normal	Transform this to, "This is our new normal." This goes back to the root of why you started this journey in the first place—being "normal" has come at a cost to the planet. Plastic is a cheap material that has quietly made its way into every part of our lives, but it comes from a non-renewable resource and is polluting our waterways and poisoning our planet. Our complacency cannot last forever. It will not be long before humans feel the effects of the plastic toxicity that is currently plaguing our sea life.
It's hard to be totally plastic-free	Transform this to, "Aim for effort, not perfection." Remember, we aren't anti plastic, we are anti single-use or "silly-use" plastic. As an engineer, I truly appreciate plastic as a material. It is lightweight, waterproof and long-lasting. There are some products for which plastic is beneficial, such as in medical uses. However, "silly-use" plastic, such as single-use plastic bags, disposable coffee cups and plastic straws, have sensible alternatives. We can make a simple switch to better alternatives so that we can save plastic for things that truly need it.

My favorite snacks come wrapped in plastic	Transform this to, "One person can make a change." See if you can turn the complaint around to find a solution. If your favorite snack comes wrapped in plastic, can you write a letter to the company that makes it to suggest alternatives? Can you make a homemade version of the snack yourself? Can you find a similar product with different packaging? Encourage your children to find creative solutions to the problem of plastic.
What about medications?	There's no transformation here. Let's be sensible: your health comes first! If you require plastic products for medical purposes, please use it. However, the medical industry can do a lot more to reduce their dependence on plastic, and this will be a challenge the industry will need to embrace in coming years. In the meantime, one thing you can do to reduce toxic landfills is to dispose of your medications responsibly. All pharmacies have a medication disposal program. Correct disposal of medications and medical waste is important, so do a quick internet search to find the right solution.

Not everyone in the family is putting in the same effort

Transform this to, "How can we make it easier for everyone?" Not everyone is going to have the same level of passion for living a zero waste life, but one thing we can do is to listen to their concerns and address them. Sometimes being heard is enough. If their effort does not change, then keep going without their help. All you can do is set a good example, and seeing you living a happy life in which there is less clutter and waste, but more happiness and freedom, most people will want to follow your lead pretty quickly. Lead with grace, and the rest will follow.

ZERO WASTE CELEBRATIONS

Today is the day to celebrate! This is a celebration of everything you've achieved so far. My favorite memories are always the festive ones in which we are surrounded by family and friends. This is a chance to show your children and others that adopting a zero waste lifestyle can be fun. Relish this moment, knowing you are doing something important for the future of your family and the planet. A great idea for celebrating your successes is to invite some guests and host a zero waste party with your family.

Here are some tips for holding a zero waste party.

1. **INVITATIONS** – Send out digital invitations and make sure they include instructions to encourage people to bring their own plates and cutlery (if you don't have a zero waste party kit). If guests are bringing a plate, encourage them to bring foods that are not packaged in plastic.

2. **MAKE YOUR OWN DECORATIONS** – Forget balloons and plastic banners—ask your kids to be creative and make some reusable decorations, such as bunting made from ribbons and cloth, or see what you can upcycle from your dry trash.

3. **ORGANIZE A WASTE STATION** – Have a bin for organic produce, a bin for recycling and a small bin for landfill. Label them accordingly so that guests can easily dispose of their waste appropriately.

4. **ENTERTAINMENT** – Find games that don't involve any plastic. This could be card games, charades or an outdoor activity. Invest in some good quality games that you can use time and time again.

PANTRY PARTY

Providing a family dinner or having guests over doesn't have to be a three-course affair. The trick is to have a few plates and recipes that you can easily rustle up without fuss. I have one set of vintage crockery and cutlery that I use daily. I never save my best crockery for special occasions—every day is a special occasion. I keep a basket of cloth napkins folded and ready, and the gathering can begin.

Here are some simple ideas for creating a feast by using what you already have in the pantry.

- PANTRY STAPLES – Olives, dips, pickled vegetables, olive oil and pesto can all easily be pulled from the pantry to create a simple charcuterie board. Buy products that are sold in glass jars, or try making your own.

- BAGUETTES – Instead of store-bought crackers, which are usually wrapped in plastic, buy a baguette from your local bakery in your own reusable packaging and cut it into thin slices as an easy and quick alternative. You can also toast the slices for a crunchy, cracker-like texture.

- FRESH FRUIT AND VEGETABLES – Freshly cut vegetable sticks such as carrot, cucumber and celery make a great starter served with dips or simply drizzled with some olive oil. Fresh fruit salad is a delicious dessert, or you could make fruit skewers using wooden or reusable stainless steel sticks.

- SIMPLE MAINS – I love freezing pizza dough that can be defrosted to make quick, easy pizzas. You can lay out whatever ingredients you have in the fridge and pantry, and everyone can add their own toppings for individual pizzas. Another easy idea is to create a simple pasta bake with vegetables you already have.

LET GUESTS PARTICIPATE

There's no shame in asking for help; in fact, most guests prefer to be given a task, as it makes them feel useful and involved in the process as well. Some simple ways to ask guests to participate include:

1. **HOME BAR** – Set up a zero waste drinks station with spirits, glass bottles of mineral water or soft drinks and cut up fruit. Ask one guest to be the bartender and make drinks for the others.

2. **BRING YOUR OWN DISH** – Plan a potluck gathering and ask guests to bring a dish. You can create themed gatherings to encourage people to try new recipes. One of my favorite themes is "zero waste food," which means asking guests to make dishes using what might be considered waste. This can include items that are close to their best-before or use-by dates, or even just finding a way to use pantry items that have been sitting unused for too long. Other themed potlucks could include an international cuisine, such as Italian nights, Indian curry nights or Chinese food. The choices are endless.

3. **SET THE TABLE** – To avoid using plastic plates, plastic cutlery and paper napkins, ask your guests to each bring their own plate, cutlery and cloth napkin. This is a great way to prevent plastic waste and it also saves you from needing to store a party's worth of extra plates, cutlery and napkins when they aren't being used.

CREATE A SHARED PARTY KIT

Create a party supplies kit for your friends and family to share. A party kit can be sourced secondhand and can include:

- plates
- cutlery
- cups
- cloth napkins
- stainless steel straws
- tablecloths
- serving platters.

This kit can be kept in a large storage container and shared among friends and family whenever there is a large gathering such as a barbecue, picnic, birthday party or other special occasion, so that no one ever needs to buy single use items again. Just ask whoever currently has the kit to bring it to the next gathering to prevent waste.

Zero waste living is about having fun! It's about making time for the things that truly matter. Use this as a day to reflect on your successes and what you can do to make things better for the next thirty days and beyond.

CONCLUSION

WHAT MATTERS MOST

I write this after a very stressful period in my life. I recently found a lump near my right ear. At first I thought it was an enlarged lymph node, but it wouldn't go away. I saw a doctor, who suggested an MRI and a biopsy. She told me that 70 percent of these parotid masses are benign, but 30 percent can be cancerous. During the days I was waiting for the results, I carried on with life in a frenzy. Answering calls from my US publisher, taking care of my daughter, preparing for my final year of medical school and writing the final chapters of this book. When the results eventually arrived, they showed it was a benign tumor but it would require major surgery to remove.

I was relieved, but at the same time I was gravely sad. All the tips I have written in this book, firstly about self-care, then about home and child care, I hadn't been applying to my own life. I was too busy surviving and I wasn't living an authentic, truly zero waste life. I couldn't sleep that night, tossing and turning, thinking about the surgery and how I would fit everything into my already very full life, and then, at 2 a.m., I fell into a heap.

I woke up with a renewed outlook and a desperate desire to change. My body was giving me signs that I could no longer push myself just to survive: I needed to thrive. I needed to slow down and take my own advice. I needed to put on my own oxygen mask first, to look after myself so I can then look after others. We are more than just machines designed to work and make profit; we are more than slaves to our families; we are more than just human shells fighting for survival. We are creative, talented, big-hearted caretakers both for our families and this planet. To thrive in this world, we must strip away the excess and focus on what matters most.

So, I am going to take my own advice and start with self-care. All the tips I outlined at the beginning of this book—having a routine for myself, removing all the excess from my daily schedule, being more present—I am going to apply rigidly, as if my life depends on it. I am also going to get back to taking care of my home and daughter in a way that is gentler for her and also for the planet. This means less consumption of "stuff," more meaningful time together, and fewer unnecessary distractions. To do this I need to apply the principles of minimalism and zero waste living in a way that encourages everyone to participate and help out. I shouldn't be the only one forging this path; this is a journey that my whole family should be engaged in, because we intrinsically care about each other and how we impact the world around us.

It starts with one person, then extends to one family. Imagine if the ripple effect extended to the eight billion people on this planet. One family alone will not tip the scales on plastic pollution, but imagine if all families, from one or two people to extended families of thirty-five or more people, all came together and did their small part. The cumulative effect would change the world.

This book is a thirty-day guide filled with practical tips on how to apply the principles of minimalism and zero waste in your daily family life. The essential ingredient is a change in mindset. People have laughed at my efforts, saying that one plastic bag isn't going to change the world, but one mind *can* change the world. The habits that you have instilled over the past thirty days represent a change in your mindset, transforming the concept of waste. Waste is not waste if you don't waste it. I hope this book has begun that change for you and also encouraged your family to see beyond the landfill. This deeper connection to the world around us is essential for human life to survive on this planet. We must start acting like caretakers, rather than just tenants on this planet we call home.

There's a growing dogma in the zero waste community that there is only *one* way to live a zero waste life. This kind of judgment is making the lifestyle inaccessible to many people. For me, a truly zero waste life is more than just a plastic-free diet. It's about not wasting away my life. It's about being generous to people and realizing there isn't just one solution to the problem.

There are zero wrong ways to live a zero waste life. I hope that, like me, you accept your mistakes and keep rereading and reusing this book. Add your own tips and tricks that suit your family's needs. I am still learning from my mistakes and learning how to live more mindfully on a daily basis. But that's what makes this journey fun—we can all embrace our creativity to think outside the plastic box. Some days are better than others, but as long as we keep trying, keep pushing for change, we are forging a path in the right direction. It's this effort over perfection that keeps it interesting. My meditation teacher calls it the flow state: the ease and grace you feel when everything is in alignment. My goal is to get to that flow state with my whole life, and it begins in the heart and in the home.

ACKNOWLEDGMENTS

This book is dedicated to all families, whether it be a family of one or one hundred. In particular, I would like to dedicate this book to my family—my husband, James, and my daughter, Vivian. James, you have taught me patience, kindness and love. I am grateful that I get to walk through life by your side. Vivian, you constantly amaze me with your intelligence and spark for life. I hope you know that Mummy will always be there for you.

To my mother, Shirley, you're the strongest person I know. I know you have passed on your kindness and strength to Vivian, and I am sure she will be so proud of these attributes. Thank you for everything you have done for our family. To my father, Henry, we are all grateful for your vivacity for life. To my brother, Alex, thank you for your humor and caring nature. To my in-laws, Yasmin and Kim, your love and support is always appreciated.

To my friends—you know who you are—2020 was a hard year for all of us, but I am so happy to have you as my chosen family. Thank you for always being there for me.

To my Penguin Random House family, Sophie Ambrose, Kathryn Knight and Louisa Maggio, and my illustrator, Melissa Stefanovski, you have helped me make this book even better than I could have imagined. Thank you.

Finally, to my Instagram family, your comments, messages and kind words of support lift my spirits whenever I have a bad day. This book would not have been possible if it weren't for you. I am endlessly grateful. Thank you. Thank you. Thank you.

A ZERO WASTE LIFE

Anita Vandyke is a qualified rocket scientist and medical doctor (Bachelor of Engineering – Aeronautical Space and Doctor of Medicine) and, most importantly, mother to Vivian. She was born in Guangzhou, China, raised in Australia, and currently splits her time between Sydney and San Francisco. Her first book, *A Zero Waste Life: In Thirty Days*, won Gold at the Nautilus Book Awards in 2019 and has been translated into seven languages. Anita writes about motherhood, zero waste living and minimalism on Instagram, at @rocket_science, and her website, anitavandyke.com.